SMOKEY
THE VERY LOUD PURRING CAT

Smokey the cat and co-writer and owner Ruth Adams

Ruth was born in a village in Derbyshire, England, and studied art at Aberystwyth and the Bournemouth and Poole College of Art and Design. Ruth and her family share their farm home with a menagerie of animals, including ponies, horses, goats, hens, bullocks, dogs, cats and goldfish.

Maybe Ruth is best-known for being the owner of Smokey, the very loud purring cat.

This story is 'written' and told by Smokey with the help of her owner, Ruth.

Smokey is a little bit woolly on the details of her previous seven homes as there is a limit to how much detail you can give in a purr and meow, so the following story is part fiction and part fact.

The two big facts are: that her enormously loud purr has been recorded in depth for the Guinness World Records for the 'Loudest Purring Domestic Cat.' The second is that their house would not be a home without the ever-present comforting purr.

SMOKEY
THE VERY LOUD PURRING CAT

By Smokey and Ruth Adams

Guinness World Records™ Record Holder
The Loudest purring domestic cat in the World

First published in Great Britain in 2011 by The Derby Books Publishing Company Limited, 3 The Parker Centre, Derby, DE21 4SZ.

ISBN 978-1-78091-000-0
Printed and bound by CPI Anthony Rowe, Chippenham.

www.smokeythepurringcat.com
twitter@PurringSmokey

Disclaimer that the first half of the book is not based on fact and is an imaginary account of her previous seven homes and is meant to have no resemblance to any persons living or dead. The accounts from joining the Adam's household are all based on fact and actually happened as described.

The Guinness World Records trademarks are used by kind permission of Guinness World Records Limited.

Photographs have been supplied by Alasdair of Digital-Nomad photography, Northamptonshire Newspapers, BBC Radio Northampton, Reverend Stephen Trott, Guinness World Records, ANV Measurement Systems, Jimoh Ayuba and Ruth Adams.

Press articles very kindly supplied by the *Northampton Chronicle and Echo* newspaper.

This story is dedicated to all charities, welfare societies and kind-hearted people who give their time for the benefit of cats and other animals.

CONTENTS

FOREWORD

I was very pleased to be asked to provide a foreword for this lovely book. It tells the story - part fiction, part fact - of Smokey, a cat who has recently risen to fame on the strength of her purr. Ruth, her owner, clearly loves not only Smokey, but also all cats, and wanted this book to assist readers to help other cats.

We often think cats purr only when they're happy. But, as one of Smokey's Cat Facts suggests, cats can purr for both good and bad reasons. On the good side, cats do purr when they are nursing kittens (like Smokey's mother), full of milk (like Smokey as a kitten), relaxed and being stroked (like Smokey) or asking us for attention or food. On the bad side, cats often purr when they are stressed, scared or in pain. Ruth helped ensure Smokey's recordings were as stress-free as possible, so I think Smokey's purring was for good reasons!

As well as purring, Smokey is able to talk, or at least type. She has even learnt some geography and politics. Thinking of animals as if they are humans is also a good and bad thing. On the one hand, it can help us to imagine what it would be like to be in their shoes (if they wore shoes) - like us, cats feel pain, stress and fear, they can get obese or hungry, they have individual likes, dislikes and wants, and they need exercise and mental stimulation. For this reason, we would not recommend keeping a cat indoors if he or she is used to going outside. But we can go too far if we treat animals like humans and not as animals. Cats often need very different things to humans, for example, they do not always like company and often do not get on with new cats (like Tiger in this story).

This creates a dilemma for people who have one cat and want to rehome another. It is lovely to take on a rescue cat and give it a second chance (or eighth in Smokey's case) in a loving home; but it would be better if cats did not need to be rehomed in the first place.

One way to avoid cats needing to be rehomed is to ensure we will keep them forever. We should only get a pet when sure we can provide a good home for the rest of their life, which requires considerable effort and expense over twenty years plus. We should microchip our cat, and ensure the database details are kept up-to-date. And we should neuter him or her. Neutering can be done from a few months old, and cats definitely do not need to have a litter first. It is a safe and quick operation (most cats go home that day), which can prevent road accidents, fighting, spraying, "yowling" when on heat, and avoids womb infections and several cancers.

You can also rehome a cat rather than buying one. Many charities, such as those below, have lovely cats like Smokey in need of good homes (although not all will be world record breakers).

9

So you can help prevent cats going through stressful times like those in Smokey's story. Smokey has landed on her feet, but many other animals need you to make sure they all have happy lives.

Dr James Yeates
Royal Society for the Prevention of Cruelty to Animals

Useful Contacts:

Advice:
RSPCA: *http://www.rspca.org.uk/allaboutanimals/pets*

Rehoming cats:

RSPCA:
http://www.rspca.org.uk/allaboutanimals/pets/rehoming

Battersea Dogs and Cats Home:
http://www.battersea.org.uk/cats/

Blue Cross:
http://www.bluecross.org.uk/2574/adopt-a-cat.html

Cats Protection:
http://www.cats.org.uk/adopt-a-cat

Wood Green:
http://www.woodgreen.org.uk/rehome/cats/rehoming_process

FOREWORD

by Diane Johnson

My friendship with Smokey's owner, Ruth, began through my volunteer work with the Northampton Branch of the UK-wide Cats Protection, hence my involvement with this heart-warming story.

Smokey – who exactly is Smokey, the Loudest purring Cat in the World? She is a gorgeous Silver Spotted British Shorthair who came into the caring home of the delightful Adams family some five years ago.

Smokey's association with Cats Protection began with a casual remark by her owner, Ruth Adams, about fund-raising for the local cats. This initial suggestion soon escalated into radio and TV interviews and, as they say, the rest is history, as Smokey is now internationally known through the *Guinness Book of World Records* due to her exceptional purr.

Smokey has proved herself to be a wonderful asset to Cats Protection by promoting the all-important neutering programme and bringing cat-ownership to the attention of many more people. We are indebted to Ruth and Mark for allowing all the subsequent filming and interviews to take place in their home.

If you are not a cat owner – I guarantee you will want to be by the time you have read this extraordinary tale – no matter what age you are! You will smile, you may even feel a little sad, BUT you will laugh too, at the way Smokey's lifestyle has been captured. If you believe in 'cat-love' – this book is for you.

Diana Johnson
September 2011

FOREWORD

I'm always incredibly purrleased to see fellow rescue felines following their dreams and heading for the stars and so I was delighted to read *Smokey the Very Loud Purring Cat* written by my noisy friend.

Smokey's first book in my cat eyes is a huge success. Its comic style and insightful titbits into the art of Smokey's talent allows all to truly respect her gift and, at the same time, leave them smiling like one of my friends from Cheshire. This book is pawfect for all ages and species, maybe even dogs as well!

I look forward to seeing Smokey following in the paw prints of my good friends, Bagpuss and Garfield and having her own TV series.

So I congratulate Smokey, the loudest cat in the world, on her wonderful book. Smokey, you really are the cat that got the cream!

Larry 'The Downing Street Cat'

Editor-in-Chief, Craig Glenday proudly holds a copy of the Guinness World Records 2012 Book.

INTRODUCTION

As the proud owner of a Guinness World Records certificate, Smokey the cat is in good company. For 57 years, the London-based company has been celebrating the most fascinating, inspiring and unique record-holders from across the planet. Whether they're mountaineers, Olympic sports stars, chainsaw jugglers or even animals such as very loud cats, Guinness World Records record holders are all part of a very exclusive club. Indeed, it was precisely because of an animal that the whole crazy enterprise began.

Guinness World Records was the result of an argument about a bird.

Back in the early 1950s, Sir Hugh Beaver, Chairman of the Guinness brewery, was enjoying a trip to County Wexford in Ireland when he and a friend had a disagreement. Sir Hugh and his buddies were taking part in a hunting party and had just missed shooting a particularly speedy golden plover.

The golden plover, said Sir Hugh, must be the fastest game bird in Europe. His fellow hunters weren't so sure. Wasn't the grouse a faster flier? argued another. Castlebridge House, the rather large country manor at which Sir Hugh was spending the night, had a grand - and in his opinion "very expensive" -

library, yet despite an intensive search, the men couldn't find a single book to solve the argument.

Sir Hugh reckoned that up and down the country, men must be having debates like this all the time, particularly in pubs and bars. And since he was in the drinks business himself and always looking for interesting new ways of selling the famous black stout, he put two and two together. What was needed, he suggested, was a way of "turning the heat of argument into the light of knowledge" - a book that pub landlords could keep behind the bar for the purpose of settling debates and selling a few pints of Guinness at the same time.

Working at the Guinness brewery at the time was a keen sportsman named Chris Chataway. An under-brewer, Chris was also a involved in amateur athletics and was the pacemaker for Roger Bannister, the runner who, on 6 May 1954 at Oxford, became the first person to run a mile in under four minutes. Chris was good friends with twin brothers Norris and Ross McWhirter, who had recently set themselves as a sports news service specializing in stats and figures. The McWhirters would be the ideal candidates for compiling Sir Hugh's compendium of facts, said Chris, and arranged for the twins to meet him.

Sir Hugh was very impressed by the identical twins, and especially with their encyclopedic knowledge. He tested them with tricky questions, all of which they answered correctly, and soon put them to work on his project. They found a small office in London's famous Fleet Street - home to the city's many newspapers- and began the task of collating facts across an enormous spectrum of topics.

A few months later, the first ever Guinness Book of Records was sent to the printers. It was a humble book - it had just one colour photograph, of Mount Everest, the world's highest peak at 8,848 m (29,029 ft) - and its simple green cover came with a beer-proof coating. Sir Hugh was terribly impressed, saying that it far exceeded his expectations, and it was suggested that the book could be sold in shops as well as given away free to some of the 80,000 or so pubs in the UK.

But the bookshops were less enthusiastic, with one major chain suggesting that they'd only ever sell a handful of copies. Of course, they were proved wrong and the first ever book, published in 1955, was an instant success. It became a Christmas bestseller that year - a position that the book has retained ever since - and it proved to be just as successful across the Atlantic, becoming a US bestseller under the title of *The Guinness Book of World Records*.

These days, of course, much has changed. The world is a very different place compared with the 1950s, and the book now has a lot more colour pictures for a start! Guinness World Records has sold 120 million books to date, making it the world's best-selling copyrighted book of all time and third only to the Bible and the Koran in total numbers sold. No longer owned by the Guinness brewery, the company name changed to Guinness World Records, and the remit widened to encompass TV shows, websites and now ebooks and apps. But the message and the mission remains the same: to research and authenticate world records and bring them to as wide an audience as possible and in a fun, engaging and entertaining way.

One of the biggest changes to occur over recent years is the shrinking of the world thanks to the Internet. It's now possible to contact just about anyone on the planet via email, and Guinness World Records now receives upwards of 65,000 claims each year. That's more than 1,000 a week! And we receive them in a vast number of languages from every country, so it's mammoth task processing every application.

But this doesn't mean we accept 1,000 records a week! Instead, we reject up to 90 per cent of applications, which means that if, like Smokey, you do receive your official Guinness World Records certificate, you are officially amazing!

(One of the weirdest claims I've ever seen is for "dog with the fewest legs"! Not only is it an odd idea for a record, the dog in question was only missing one leg. A quick Google search revealed that three-legged dogs are not uncommon and that Queen Elizabeth had a corgi with two legs (it had pram wheels in place of its back legs! Thankfully, I couldn't find a dog with just one leg...)

The nature of record claims has also changed over the years, as has our opinion of what makes a good record. In the past, for example, we used to accept claims for heaviest pets. We'd be sent video footage of lardy Labradors and portly pussies and marvel at how massive these pets could grow. Then owners desperate for record recognition began overfeeding their animals and it got to the stage when we had to turn away all requests for heaviest pets - a process we call "resting" a record.

Other categories rested over the years include riding horses over great distances, blood sports such as bullfighting and fox hunting, and such exotic activities as camel wrestling and elephant polo. We also take a dim view of many circus-related animal achievements where we suspect that there might be cruelty involved. As the former Editor of Animals Animals Animals magazine - and yes, it was about animals! - I know just how much people love and respect their pets, and want to be sure that animals are shown the same consideration as any human.

And so to Smokey the cat, who has honoured me with the request of contributing these few words. I'm more than happy to accept - it's not every day a cat asks you to write a chapter for its autobiography! (To be honest, neither is it every day that a cat writes an autobiography!) It also gives me something to do as I fly to South Korea on yet another record research trip. Staff at every level of Guinness World Records are trained as record adjudicators, and we get to visit the most fantastic places to meet the most amazing characters. On my last trip, for example, I visited the USA to measure a miniature donkey in Florida and a tiny cat in California.

Smokey was the first cat to set the record for loudest purr, and joins a list of other marvellous moggies. Recent additions to our cat-alogue of records include the Maine coon Mymains Stewart Gilliga (aka Stewie), the longest cat in the world at 48.5 inches from nose to tail - enormous when you consider the typical cat length of 18 inches). At the other end of the ruler is the 19-cm-long (7.5-in) Tinker Toy, the shortest cat by length that ever lived; and the shortest by height is currently the utterly adorable Fizz Girl, the aforementioned Californian cat who lives with her feline family on a ranch alongside a menagerie of parrots, dogs and horses - she reached just 15.24 cm (6 in) to the shoulder!

Other cat-egories (sorry, couldn't resist) in the records database include longest whiskers (19 cm or 7.5 in, belonging to Missi, another Maine coon, this time from Finland), the cat with the most toes (Jake the rescue cat from Ontario in Canada, who clawed his way to fame with a record 28 toes) and one of my all-time favourites: the most expensive pet wedding! To achieve this latter record, the wealthy owners of diamond-eye cats Ploy and her well-groomed groom Phet forked out more than $16,000 for their nuptials in Thailand... complete with white dress, Rolls Royce cars, wedding cake and even a dowry of $60,000! Even more oddly, the best man was a parrot. The maid of honour? An iguana, of course!

And on the decibel scale, how does Smokey's record compare with her noisy neighbours in the Guinness World Records book? Well, with a purr of 67.7 decibels, Smokey's a long way from being the loudest animal of them all (fin whales and blue whales sing at up to 188 decibels), and it will come as no surprise to hear that a dog can bark at up to 108 decibels (Daz the white German shepherd in June 2009). But purring is usually a gentle murmur at around 25 decibels - not a roar as loud as a passing airplane!

Talking of which, I'm about to land and need to sign out now. I hope you enjoy reading about Smokey as much as we've enjoyed researching her record. And remember, if you've got a talented terrapin or a brilliant budgie, let us know about it -

visit us at **www.guinnessworldrecords.com** and tell us all about it and your pet might even make it into the record books alongside Smokey! Good luck...

Craig Glenday
Editor-in-Chief
Guinness World Records

PS, and if you're wondering, the grouse can reach speeds in flight of up to 100 kph (63 mph) - so sorry, Sir Hugh, you were wrong - this is faster than the plover!

BEHIND THE SOFA

I am tired, so very tired after filming; it has been a very long day and I want to hide from the world, or at least from my family, and they will never find me behind the sofa.

I ache so much I can barely lift my head from the fluffy carpet. I am totally drained, my ribs hurt and my throat is sore. I am so stressed and frightened. I don't want to play anymore, let alone eat. Maybe if I could hide for just a few more hours, I will feel better for tomorrow.

'Smokey, where are you?' the call comes from the kitchen. 'Smokeee, Smokeeee'. The calls get more urgent now.

I can hear two sets of feet shuffling around as Ruth, my owner, and Diana, her friend, are searching for me.

Normally I love a good game of hide and seek to keep myself amused but today I am too pooped to enjoy how well I'm hiding. The footsteps draw closer and the inevitable 'I've found her' was declared.

Oh no, just leave me alone, I surrender – I thought – you win!

Ruth's arms reach down and scoop me up like a little ball and wrap themselves around me in a gentle loving cuddle, like a blanket they comfort me and I feel the love. Happy again, I relax and then without opening my mouth a magic rumbling starts tickling in my throat and my rib cage begins to quiver and vibrate and all that tension is released in a breath of rumbling purr. That feels so much better I am relaxing already. I think more calmly, breathe more deeply and go into a purr-like trance. The louder I purr the better it feels. I am totally addicted to purring as it makes me feel so good.

My name is '**Smokey**' and I am probably the world's loudest-purring cat. I am becoming a bit of an International Celebrity.

The volume level of my purr has been compared to an aeroplane, hairdryer, food blender, vacuum cleaner and lawn mower. I know I'm loud, but I am just a very happy cat and can't stop telling people how much I love them.

It's a hard life being a celebrity cat. I carry out purr-training sessions daily to encourage me to purr. This is done more to reassure my owner that I can deliver the required purr on demand.

Only three months ago my life consisted of a regular routine of eating, purring, sleeping, stroking, garden excursions and more sleeping, and the main focus of my attention and aspiration was to eat. Now I have found there is more to life. I have discovered the art of International purring. I love the attention but it can be very tiring.

This afternoon I finished filming with the ABC Television news programme *Good Morning America*. The shooting took around four hours and a lot of organising for the team of five humans who turned up. I was totally overwhelmed, but I always try to please, so for those four hours I purred continuously and my throat is so dry I feel all burned out. My purr has dried up to a splutter and all I can do is cough and dribble. But I did well today. I can rest now.

The attention of the International media can be very stressful and so demanding. I rather stumbled across stardom and applying for the Guinness World Records record for the World's 'loudest purring domestic cat'.

If it is possible to accidently apply for a Guinness World Records record then I did this, and this is my story: the tale of how a seven times rehomed rescue cat found her voice and purred her story of happiness around the world.

'The smallest feline is a masterpiece'
Leonardo da Vinci

HAPPY BEGINNINGS

I was born around 12 years ago in 1999 in the county of Northamptonshire. My mother was very kind and I loved snuggling up next to her. I had a sister and two brothers, and I was always the playful one in charge of the games. Our mother lovingly licked us all over with her rough tongue to clean our fur and she continually purred to us in a low soothing voice. I loved listening to her rumbling purr telling us to drink more of the milk from her soft tummy. I soon learnt to purr back to her and she would roll over to let me access her milk. These were very happy memories. Sometimes I feel a little sad that I can't return to those contented times. I do miss my mummy and our basket next to the cream Aga cooker. The cooker was always warm and emitted the most wonderful smells, it made everything seem cosy and safe.

I never knew or met my father and my mother could only tell me a little about him after their rather quick date in the garden a few months before I was born. I am told he was a very handsome Pedigree British Shorthair cat and he had appeared on television in an advertising campaign about washing powder. So being a celebrity cat was obviously in my blood.

When I was eight weeks old I was told it was time for me to leave home and find my own way in the big wide world with a new owner. This was a very traumatic time for me. I did not want to leave mummy. Prospective owners came to meet us and with my very large eyes and very happy purr I was first to be chosen.

MY SECOND HOME

My second home was with a young lady, Karen, who was a nurse. She was very kind to me but I saw very little of her as she worked very long hours at the hospital. I was left alone with my scratching post, litter tray and a red and grey padded mouse to amuse myself. I was lonely, so very lonely so I purred out loudly and hoped someone would hear me and come and play. I missed my mother, brothers and sister.

Karen always stroked me when she came home and gave me a big cuddle. She knew I was lonely and one day she came home very excited carrying the cat carrier and inside was a small black cat named 'Sooty'.

The basket was opened and a very shy black female emerged and ran straight past without even looking at me and then dived headlong into the sofa underneath the cushions and there she remained. Some friend she's going to be I thought sadly to myself, and even worse she may try to steal my food. I did not want another cat on my territory I wanted my owner just to dote on me.

Sooty and I soon established some ground rules. She kept to her side of the room out of sight hiding somewhere and I sat on the most comfortable chair near the radiator waiting to be stroked. It was my place to adorn the settee and chairs, be stroked by my owner and purr as warranted by my position as 'top cat'!

Don't get me wrong I enjoyed the company of another cat and as long as she learnt to respect me then all was well.

Life was good and I was becoming settled and would purr loudly because I was so happy. Karen felt guilty about leaving me on my own for so long that she always came home with tasty treat sticks and chews for me. I purred to say thank you. I was beginning to learn that when I purred I could control Karen's actions. I could tell her to come over and stroke me if I increased the volume and then I'd make it a little shriller and demanding, by that she would know that I was hungry. This was a brilliant discovery. I had discovered how to train humans. I felt very pleased with myself and confident with the power it gave me.

One summer evening the telephone rang and Karen jumped up sharply knocking me off her knee as she rose. I was a bit annoyed but managed to land on my feet. I could sense her excitement and how her nature suddenly changed from us sharing a quick nap to her tingling with energy. She started to giggle and shriek and I remember her saying.

'Well it's a date then!'

I had no idea how much those words were going to change my life.

The boyfriend had arrived on the scene. Karen no longer cuddled and stroked me on the sofa as she now had a new human companion and he was definitely not a cat type of person. A cat can tell, you know, if a person is uncomfortable around them, it's one of our many extra senses. We can pick up and tune in to feelings and that is why we are such excellent companions.

This could be a competition for Karen's attention. I increased my purr level a few notches; this was becoming an emergency!

Even if the boyfriend was not around Karen's attention was no longer just for me. I felt I was losing control. I felt like a discarded toy, and I was no longer of interest to her and it upset me so much. Now that 'Mr Boyfriend' had arrived Karen was out late and sometimes never returned home at night. I was worried, very worried and occasionally we even missed a meal. This was very serious.

Karen's friends came over one evening and suddenly she said 'I've got some wonderful news! I'm getting married! My boyfriend, Keith, proposed last night and we are going to travel and see the world together'. Karen's friends hugged and congratulated her.

Good News? How can this be good news I thought? What's going to happen to me and Sooty?

This was really distressing. I began to feel depressed and did not feel much like purring.

The answer to my question was a sideways move to the house next door. I could not believe it. I had been the perfect purring companion to Karen for four years. I had done nothing wrong apart from the occasional hairball left behind a cushion discreetly. I did not shred the furniture. I WAS A GOOD CAT. I did not deserve this. Suddenly I was no longer family but a disposable item. I had no idea just how disposable I was going to be.

'A cat has absolute emotional honesty: human beings, for one reason or another, may hide their feelings, but a cat does not.'
Ernest Hemingway

30

SPARE RIBS

This was going to be my third home. Karen asked Paul, our human neighbour, to adopt us. Karen was very purrrrsuasive.

He reluctantly agreed.

I had my concerns and reservations from the start; I did not think our neighbour could really appreciate what a superrrrrrb cat I was and how lucky he was to have me! I was not happy about this arrangement and I felt very annoyed that Karen had not consulted me and why on earth did she need to see the world. I have been all the way down to the Recreation Ground and back and I can assure her that travel is not all it's cracked up to be.

We moved next door with Paul. I had seen him many times before in his garden so he was not a stranger to me. He made Sooty and I feel very welcome but his cat, Tiger, was not at all happy about our arrival and spat 'go away' straight in my face when he saw me. I could not believe it, he was so rude. I was shocked. He arched his back, and ruffled his fur so it stood on end. Tiger was a feral cat in a former life and he knew how to intimidate unwelcome visitors on his patch. Tiger was a territorial monster. Were

Karen and Paul mad to imagine that Sooty and I could possibly share a sofa with Tiger?

Paul worked very long hours at his BBQ steak house called, somewhat unoriginally, 'Paul's BBQ house'. However, when he came home he always brought tasty left-overs back for my supper wrapped in a red serviette. The T-bones, ribs and steak gristle could be a challenge to chew as they were a bit difficult for my thin sharp teeth, but they were very tasty.

My favourite had to be the succulent sweet tasty gammon basted with honey. I got to know the whole menu and we three cats would sit by the door expectantly arguing over who would eat what of the offerings. Well, to be honest there was not much arguing as Tiger simply hissed 'I am having' and Sooty and I rather meekly would say 'alright then'. You don't argue with an angry, tabby cat who has some serious issues. Tiger really did find it difficult to accept that I needed to be the 'top cat' in the household.

It was during my time spent at Paul's that I developed my passion for good food. I really do appreciate good quality dining and won't purr if anything less is placed in my bowl. I am a distinguished connoisseur of good taste.

Paul started his BBQ Bar 20 years ago and for all those years he had basted and grilled and sizzled chops and ribs. Paul was dedicated to his business and when he was at home he was so exhausted he fell asleep in front on the television watching sport in his armchair with a bottle or can of beer. I used to feel comforted by his rhythmical loud snoring when he dozed off. In fact, I think I have to credit him for teaching me further purr rumbling technique.

A year passed and we all settled in to our daily routines and Tiger eventually tired of trying to be nasty when he realised that we were not going away.

Then one day disaster struck. Paul did not come home from work and the sitting room had a deathly hush. I circled around the mat not sure what to do with myself. I was suddenly gripped by insecurity. I hated any change to my routine.

The next morning the key turned in the lock and a lady I have never met before entered the house. She was sobbing very loudly and was bent over as though she did not have the strength to stand up. We three cats kept our distance hiding from behind the sofa. Tiger peered round to spy. The lady in the red coat busied herself rummaging through the desk by the window. She was very agitated and such sadness surrounded her. She picked up the telephone and tapped in some numbers from the diary she had retrieved from the desk. We strained to hear what was said.

'Hello is that Sue? I have some terrible news for you', she explained.

'I am sorry, so very sorry to have to tell you, that Paul died last night while at work. The doctors say it was a brain tumour which he had had for some time. We are all totally in shock. I know this is not a good time to mention it but Paul had three cats and we need to find them new homes.' She put the telephone down and, still crying started to sort through further papers in the desk.

I felt desperately sad. A human life was, indeed, short. I was going to be homeless again. I was no longer a kitten or young cat and nobody would want to take on three older cats. After a large number of telephone calls a 'temporary foster home' was eventually found for us. The decision was made to separate Tiger from us as it was felt as a single cat he would have a greater chance of adoption.

LIFE BEHIND BARS

Nothing can ever prepare a cat for leaving a comfortable home and being placed in a soulless pen in a cat shelter. I felt I was being placed in jail for a crime I did not commit. My offence was being an older cat when everyone wants to adopt kittens. I cried.

My world and Sooty's now consisted of a wire enclosure which was approximately three feet wide by five feet long. I could walk the perimeter in one minute if I took a leisurely dawdle. At one end of the pen a wooden ramp led up to a raised and enclosed sleeping area with a blue blanket. A couple of cat toys were left discarded on the hard concrete floor. At the front left of the cage and in full public view was a litter tray. How could any self-respecting cat maintain her dignity when attending to business with humans watching? The plastic empty food dish and water bowl were placed on the other side of the door.

There were further cells on either side of us both with inmates in. The prisoner to the right was deaf so that made any conversation difficult and the couple of cats to the left were permanently locked in a hissing domestic argument with each other. I felt very scared, sad and lonely for human company. Sooty said very little and hid at the back, whimpering.

I watched as other convicts had been released, when they amused humans who walked down the block, so I knew I needed to draw attention to myself to get out of here with Sooty.

My cunning plan was to make my big eyes look friendly and purr loudly at any prospective family whose attention I could catch. If I did not like the look of them, I told Sooty we should hide together at the back of the pen. The potential owners filed past, unaware that I was the one doing the choosing.

'What greater gift than the love of a cat?'
Charles Dickens

'Animals are such agreeable friends – they ask no questions, they pass no criticisms.'
George Elliot

FAMILY LIFE

Then I saw my purrfect family. They all looked very relaxed and had two young children, a boy and a girl. The small girl, dressed in pink, ran straight to the pen door and looked at me with admiration. She was so excited that I knew I would be the centre of her attention. I padded forward and purposely purred my heart out.

'Daddy I want this one, please daddy. I want this one. She's friendly' the little girl pleaded with her father.

I am leaving here after a sentence of only six weeks, released for good behaviour. Welcome to home number five I thought.

We were a very happy household and I knew that this time I had landed on my paws and found a suitable pad. It felt so good to be stroked and fussed over, although it was not always easy providing free child minding service. The young girl, Emily, was five years old and never tired of playing with me. Emily loved dolls, especially girly dolls with pink floral dresses. For the record everyone I do not like pink. I soon became her favourite toy dressed in my pink bonnet being tucked into a pink toy pram and being pushed around the garden. This was seriously uncool.

I am so thankful that embarrassing photographs were not taken and published in this book. Sooty never joined in these jolly jaunts preferring to perfect her hiding skills.

When not being turned into a baby doll I would hope to catch a few quick cat naps. Sleep is very important to us cats; in fact, a truly contented cat will sleep blissfully for half the day. John, Emily's older brother, aged seven, had other ideas. Santa Claus had given him a shiny yellow bulldozer with a large sand-shovelling bucket on the front. John took great delight in waking me up sharply every time I comfortably dozed by driving his bulldozer towards me at full pelt, crashing in to me. I think my heart left my body repeatedly and I am sure I lost at least six of my nine lives from this game. I decided the only way to avoid this sharp awakening was not to sleep on the floor. I chose a sunny window sill for my new bed, which Emily very kindly made into a bed with a pink cot blanket and cushion. A good window sill was now my preferred sleeping place.

My purr was beginning to develop well and grew louder and louder. The more attention I received the louder I purred. I purred LOUDER and LOUDER and LOUDER: I was so happy!

'Shut that damn cat up' Emily, 'I am on the telephone' and 'I can't hear myself think' snapped her father, Tom. He was beginning to get very cross.

'That cat's annoying me' he grizzled.

'What's that noise?' asked Tom's friend on the other end of the telephone. 'I can't believe it's a cat making that entire racket. It sounds like an angry dove.'

I grinned and smirked to myself. I think they knew I was around. I loved the attention, I felt very important. Despite my loud and sometimes annoying purr, the parents adored me as I provided a 24-hour child amusement service. This was not my chosen profession but I must say that I adapted very well and I was always destined to be the centre of attention. I could happily live here. I knew my home here would always be secure because the parents really appreciated that John and Emily were so happy with me.

I was wrong.

Things were going well until Tom sneezed not once but three times in a row. Whenever he came near me he sneezed loudly. I didn't find it a very pleasant response to my purr.

'Those blasted cats' shouted the man. 'They've got to go. I am allergic to them'. Tom picked both of us up and we were pushed outside on to the wet doorstep. 'Go and play outside girls, we'll feed you later when it stops raining. You are doorstep cats now. You need to live outside', he sneezed and closed the door.

Not again I thought. Please not again. I cried. This was utter madness and totally unbelievable. It was drizzling with rain and my fur was getting wet. I was an indoor type of girl. This must be a mistake I thought. I felt sure that Emily would come out in a minute to play. I sat by the door and waited and waited. I tried purring to invite her out to play but my purr level was muted by depression and the endless rain which was now falling heavier. Still the blue door did not open. I tapped on the door with my paws, gently to start with using one leg and when that did not get a response I pounded the door with the full force of both paws. I was ignored.

A 'doorstep cat' – I was not sure I liked the sound of that. I do not suit the wet fur look, it makes my whiskers go curly and I resemble a drowned rat. I am not the sort of girl who rummages in dustbins; I am a warm radiator type of girl. I need my creature comforts. Why me, why does nobody want me? I sobbed uncontrollably.

I need a cosy home to purr in.

Sooty slinked away and took up residence in the garden shed; I despondently followed her grimacing as I pushed my way through the cobwebs in the broken window. 'Help' I meowed pitifully. I had lost my purr and my home. I looked out of the dirty window, up towards the heavens hoping for some signs of brightness but the sky looked remorsefully grey, heavy and depressing. The clouds seemed as sad as I was and we cried together.

Two hours later the rain still had not stopped and the door partially opened and our food bowls were placed on the doorstep. I waited till the shower eased and ventured out to investigate. Inside the bowls, the once-dry cat biscuits now floated like bobbing sponges in a pool of water. I decided that I was not hungry after all and walked away.

After three weeks of being 'door step' cats our perfect loving family decided to find us a new home, so they returned us to the rescue shelter we came from only five months earlier.

CAT FACT

If you sneeze whenever you're near cats, it may not be the cat hair making you sneeze but the saliva that remains on their fur from licking themselves clean, or their dander/skin particles. Bathing a cat regularly will help people with allergies tolerate it better.

A FEELING OF
DÉJÀ VU

Have you ever had the feeling that you've been somewhere before. The French call it déjà vu and I have definitely been here before and had not planned on coming back.

'Welcome back girls', the lady said enthusiastically.

'What have you been up to? Have you been upsetting people?' she asked. 'We were not expecting to see you both back here so soon. I am afraid your previous pen is now occupied but I have another one around the corner which will do very nicely'.

'Do! Do I look like a cat who wants to make do!' I hissed to myself.

Back to jail. I need one of those get out of jail free cards from a Monopoly game. Was I destined to spend my life here? I hated having other cats, and their constant smell, around me. I paced around the confines of my pen feeling very depressed.

When visiting day came on Sunday I knew the drill. My plan was the same as before but this time I was not choosy about who took us home I just wanted to get out of here. The first few visitors who walked passed our pen did not even look at us.

Then a young lady in a short denim skirt and spiky brightly orange coloured hair arrived. I was mesmerised by the hair: I had never seen a human with orange tabby stripes before. The orange lady was called Alice and she smiled straight at me. My heart melted and I purred, pleading with her to take me home. It worked and we were on the move again. Arrangements were made, questions were asked and all was ready for our next move.

CAT FACT

Pregnant women should avoid coming in contact with cat litter as they can catch a protozoan disease called toxoplasmosis. This may cause illness in humans and possible birth defects in the unborn. Pregnant women and those with a poor immune system should not touch a cat litter box.

CAT FACT

Cats have a flexible backbone and this is why when they fall they are able to twist and fall on their feet.

CAT FACT

At night a cat can see six times better than a human.

BUT MUM!

'We don't want a cat' are not the welcoming words a cat wants to hear when she is carried across the threshold into her new home.

'What on earth have you done? You'll have to take them straight back tomorrow. We can't afford them and we live on a busy road. What on earth were you thinking of?' shouted Alice's mum from across the room. Sooty and I trembled in the cat carrier. We were scared.

'But mum! You promised I could have a pet when I was 18 years old and started working, I am not taking them back' Alice replied. Her voice was sounding shaky and very emotional. This was not the happy response I had dreamed of. I needed to purr to get my point across. So I PURRED.

'What is that noise? What have you got in there?' questioned Alice's mother.

'She's purring at you mum, she loves you' replied Alice. 'Please give her a chance'.

A lot of discussion went on and the cat basket was left near the door. They shouted so loudly that they could not hear my purr pleading with them to 'please love me'. Eventually the voices calmed down and a decision was made to give it a trial: which meant Alice would be allowed to keep us both, but in her bedroom upstairs.

Sadly this was not a happy time for me and I felt stressed and saddened by the growing tension which was developing between Alice and her parents. I instantly knew that this was not going to be a long-term loving home for Sooty and myself. Things were never going to work out or improve, and half a dozen hairballs, three bags of cat litter and a shredded dressing table leg later, Alice's mum could see life was not going well.

'They have to go back honey, it's cruel to keep them shut up in your room and your dad does not want cats all over the house. I do wish you'd talked to us first.' Alice's mother said calmly to her daughter.

'They are my cats, mum, I love them and they love me' Alice was digging in for a strong argument.

The 'take the cats back or you must leave' statement almost seemed inevitable.

Alice spread the newspapers out over her bedroom floor and circled in pen her intended lodgings. For once I sat quietly not daring to purr while she telephoned various landlords who were advertising accommodation to let.

'No cats,' 'definitely no cats', 'no pets allowed' they all said. They were not welcoming.

Eventually Alice found us a small bedsit flat and I moved in to my seventh home with her and Sooty. The initial air of excitement soon dwindled and Alice was feeling depressed. This place was cold and damp and because it was on the fourth floor, when I tried to look out of the window all I could see was another rooftop and part of a tree top. The window sill was very narrow and so I was unable to sleep on it and unlike most cats I am afraid of heights.

I knew Alice was only trying to help me so I muzzled her and purred kindly. After only two weeks Alice was running out of money, our cat litter had not been changed and I was hungry. Things were bad.

With her eyeliner smudged from crying Alice loaded us back into the cat basket and returned us to a different animal rescue shelter called NANNA (Northamptonshire Animals Needing Nurturing and Adoption).

THE SEARCH FOR AN OLDER HOUSE CAT

Meanwhile in a different part of Northamptonshire, Jordan (9) and Amy his sister (7) were also crying because their kittens, Archie and Bandit had both died. Archie had been killed by a fox, and Bandit had been run over on the very busy road near to the farmhouse where they lived.

'That's the fourth of our kittens to be killed on the road. It's not fair' Amy sobbed. 'I love my cats. Why does it always happen to my cats?'

'I am so sad. I really liked Archie, he was my friend' said a very unhappy Jordan.

'I don't think we should get any more cats' said Jordan's father, Mark. 'It's too upsetting for the family when they die, we can't stop the cats wandering across the road.'

'How about a house cat?' suggested Ruth, the children's mother? 'A lot of people keep cats who never venture outside, so maybe we could find a house cat'

'I am not sure that is a good idea' uttered Mark.

Well, Ruth was on a mission, she was determined to find a replacement cat for her children. She rang several of the rehoming shelters and explained what she was looking for.

'I need to find an older house cat who is good with dogs, children and will be happy to spend most of its time living indoors as we live next to a very busy road.'

It seemed a simple enough wish list but few of the rehome shelters were able to guarantee that their cats would be good with children, dogs, and that they would be happy remaining indoors. Many of the cats in their care had suffered lots of mental and physical trauma and were looking for a quiet life rather than a busy family home.

When NANNA received the telephone enquiry they immediately recommended me and my rather shy pal Sooty, as they knew we were children friendly.

Ruth and the children were so excited that they couldn't wait for the weekend to visit the rehome shelter at Irthlingborough, in Northamptonshire. They were only open on Sundays and Wednesdays. The family wanted to be sure of being first there, so arrived an hour before the gates were opened and sat on a tartan car rug strewn across the pavement. They all munched chocolate bars and drank squash while they waited.

The kennel maid greeted them and explained that there were several cats that would be suitable but that Ruth and the family needed to look at all the cats at the shelter before making up their minds.

Visiting day and time for the purring routine again. I saw the family enter the garden where my pen was located, but then they turned to the right and went into the wooden shed which housed the cats in individual cages. I pushed my face against the wire wall, straining to get a sight of them. 'I'm over here I thought'.

When they reappeared, they headed towards me chattering and discussing which of the cats they preferred. I was jealous. My turn now and time for a mega life-changing purr. I took a deep breath and let rumble my happy greetings. I kept watching them as they entered our pen. It was a tight squeeze with five of us in there. I walked towards the children with my tail carried high in greeting and to my surprise the boy pushed me to one side and reached down and picked up the hiding and trembling black Sooty.

'I always wanted a black cat' he exclaimed.

'Which cat would you like to take home Amy?' Ruth asked Amy.

'I don't know' replied Amy 'they are all nice. I can't decide. I want to give all of them a home' she hesitated and thought for a few moments and then said 'but that silver one in here has a very cute purr.' She said. 'I want the little black one' reminded Jordan.

So that was it – we were selected because of Sooty. At least it justified me having had her tag along for so many years.

Thankfully the family passed the home inspection. We were a perfect match. Hopefully my eighth home would be my last one. I was tired of a nomadic life. I was ready to settle down.

I loved my new home; they had a warm fire and comfortable sofas. Sooty was still very shy and tried to hide among the cushions if she heard voices approach. The new family were frightened that they were going to sit on her by accident.

I settled into a very happy routine, everything felt so perfect. I had a few issues with fleas which had followed me from the rehome shelter and my habit of placing hairballs on the furniture had caused me some trouble a few times. It's not my fault if I have hair stuck in my throat and tummy, and if I'm choking then I am going to cough it out. I need daily grooming.

The children took turns to feed and brush us and Ruth was responding well to my purr requests for attention. I could get her to stand up and walk across the room towards me simply by purring. I was so happy. I loved my purr power.

As a cat, I do not belong to any religion, but on one day I found myself attending a special Pets Service organised by our local church. This was rather funny as the vicar had asked Ruth to bring along some of the farm animals to make things a little bit more interesting. So the decision was made to also bring along Tilley, the goat, Buttercup, the hen and Buster, the dog.

Ruth walked the goat towards the churchyard across the field as Tilley was too large to fit in the car with us and the rest of the family. Everybody knows that goats can climb, so it never occurred to Ruth that there would be a problem in getting the goat in to the churchyard over the wooden style.

Unfortunately, that day was obviously a non-climbing day for Tilley, the goat, and so Ruth had to carry the awkward animal over the style in her long flowing skirt, much to the amusement of all the villagers watching from a marquee. I am only 12in high and the obstacle was three times my height but I could have cleared that wooden style with no problem at all.

What was wrong with Tilley? She could have stepped over it blindfolded! The goat had not finished humiliating the family just yet. Amy wished to hold the goat's lead rope. This was a bad idea; a hungry goat and trestle tables bowing under the weight of cucumber sandwiches and colourful cakes. Tilley obviously believed it was a help yourself buffet and did just that, heartily tucking into the feast. After all, the tables were at an inviting goat-head height…

The onlookers would have been horrified but they were too busy laughing at the spectacle of Amy being dragged around by a very enthusiastic hungry goat.

The vicar preached and we sang the hymn *All things bright and beautiful, all creatures Great and Small* and the hen decided to join in. Buttercup was perched next to the vicar on Amy's friend's knee wrapped in a towel. I am used to drowning out people with my purr but I am not sure what the vicar thought about being out-clucked.

For once in my life I uttered nothing, I was frozen to the spot on Ruth's lap. Either side of me two large dogs were slobbering watching my every move. I knew I would be history if they came any closer. Some very sensible humans came and stroked me and commented on what a beautiful cat I was. I have to say I agree with them. The sermon ended and the vicar blessed us all.

We spent a lot of money on the raffle and we won a pot of

home made strawberry jam and triumphantly we returned home with the prize. The goat, having gorged herself on all the cakes, was even more reluctant to attempt the style challenge on the return journey.

Life on the farm is fun; I have joined a menagerie of dogs, hens, ponies, goats, cows and goldfish. I spend most of my time snoozing on the window sill by the door which has been bedded down with cushions so that I am comfortable, there are no toy yellow bulldozers in sight waiting to run me down.

Three years pass and Sooty and I are so happy, I can't stop purring. We have found our forever home and it's wonderful. I can't stop telling my owners how much I love them. I purr and I purr.

'Shut that cat up!' is often shouted in our house, but the family have come to realise it's just my way of me telling them I love them.

'Get that cat out of my office', 'put the cat in another room', 'there is cat hair everywhere'. Every relationship has its good and bad days. Maybe, I occasionally admit to getting on their nerves a little, but at least I know they will not dispose of me. After three years I can now say I feel settled. I am going nowhere.

THE VERY UNWELCOME INTRUDER

One day an unwelcome intruder arrived at the farm, in the shape of a wandering white, female stray cat. The little white cat was shivering and lay curled up in a ball underneath the children's climbing frame. She was acting the role of a starving, helpless and needy cat, but I could see straight through it. That cat was planning to wangle her way into my home and take over my cushion on the window sill. What a nerve this cat had! Just turning up and taking up Ruth's attention. I was jealous and this was my territory.

My owner used to have a white cat when she was a child and somehow she made an imaginary connection with this cat and felt compelled to help. Why could it not have been a brown tabby or a ginger cat? I have spent many years purrrrfecting my purr and settling into my home and I do not wish to share it with any more cats. I was cross, very cross. I felt like hissing and not purring.

'Puss Puss, Would you like something to eat? You poor thing you look starving. Are you hurt?' Ruth asked, approaching the stray cat with my food bowl in her hand.

'Yes I am hungry and I am right behind you' I thought grumpily. Ruth could not hear my thoughts or see me hissing through the window, so she carried on trying to coax the intruder forward.

My owner needed reminding on where her loyalties should lie, so I decided that I should remind her by regurgitating a hairball where she normally sat on the sofa, and having a shredding session on the upholstery. Wow that feels better I thought, purring with glee at my naughtiness.

Puss Puss in the meantime had wolfed down a sachet of my food and was rubbing her head and body against my owner's legs. She latched herself on to Ruth and stalked her around the farm becoming a following white shadow.

Ruth felt that this friendly cat must belong to somebody and so decided to try and reunite them. She put up a few 'cat found posters' around the neighbourhood and searched on the internet to see if any white female cats had been lost. We drew a blank. The next move was to take the cat to the local Abington Vets, to find out if the cat had been micro-chipped. Some owners ask vets to insert a microchip into their cat's neck which has details of their home. The microchip is about the size of a grain of rice.

Unfortunately, Puss Puss did not have a magic chip to reunite her with her former owner. The vets had further bad news for Ruth. The shocking news was that the cat was about to have kittens and it would be in the best interest of the cat if she was left at the surgery for rehoming. I was so pleased when my owner came back with an empty basket. I was enjoying my gloating at having despatched the intruder. But two days later, my celebrations were cut short when I heard Ruth on the telephone talking to the Animals in Need Rescue Centre where the cat had been placed by the vets. It turned out that Puss Puss, this had now become her name, had not been pregnant after all, and Ruth was making arrangements to collect her from the shelter and bring her 'home' after she had been micro-chipped.

Puss Puss was not an indoor type of girl, which was a least one saving grace and she took up residence in an empty stable among some hay bales and horse rugs. She proved herself to be a good hunter and took over the role of 'Vermin Controller' on the farm. She preferred to eat her meals fresh and her favourite was rabbit.

I amused myself by glaring at Puss Puss if she came near to the house. I scowled and hissed at her if I met her outside but she did not react to me at all. I was cross. This was my territory. My family had become rather attached to her and I was beginning to have to come to terms with the fact that she was going to be a sister cat.

Then suddenly, now sooner than she had arrived on the farm, she magically vanished. Brilliant – life was good. So she's gone, why the fuss? I thought. She chose to leave. Maybe she has gone to her proper home? I had to watch as more posters were printed and pinned up again around the villages.

The lost cat action plan sprung into motion. It was through her efforts to find the white cat, again, that Ruth was introduced to Diana Johnson, a volunteer helper with the Northampton branch of the British feline charity Cats Protection.

Diana advised Ruth to contact the local BBC Radio station as they sometimes put out lost cat bulletins. Diana and Ruth became good friends. I also liked her because, as soon as she saw me, she exclaimed, 'what a beautiful cat'. She is obviously a good judge.

'She has an incredible purr. Is she normally this loud? asked Diana.

'She is a very happy cat' Ruth explained.

A couple of weeks passed and the telephone rang with news that the cat had been found. I'd hoped that my owner would have forgotten the white cat. Arrangements were made to collect her at 6pm that evening.

Just before they were due to depart, the telephone rang again, but this time it was a veterinary surgery located in the centre of the town on the line.

'We have Puss Puss here, would you like to collect her?' said the caller enthusiastically.

'But that's totally impossible as I am due to pick her up in a few minutes from elsewhere. Are you sure it is her?' questioned Ruth. '100 per cent we have Puss Puss, we have read her microchip. She has been living at a lorry haulage depot for the last two weeks and the drivers were worried they would run her over so they brought her in to us. They were feeding her sausage and bacon from their staff canteen'.

So 'Puss Puss' came back, and all due to that tiny little invisible micro-chip embedded in her neck.

Ruth and Diana were overjoyed. I can't say I was purring with joy alongside them.

The explanation for her adventures was that she probably had jumped in the back of a lorry visiting the farm and ended up at the lorry haulage depot 12 miles away in the centre of town. She was always hunting rabbit in the strangest of locations.

Ruth and Diana contacted BBC Radio Northampton to give them the good news: the cat had been found, and to mention the benefits of micro chipping your pet. A letter to the *Northampton Chronicle & Echo* paper followed with the microchip advice. Following the letter to the local paper about Puss Puss's return we received an interesting call.

'I'm calling about the white cat' said the lady.

Oh no! An impending custody battle thought Ruth.

'The cat used to live with us in the village.' The lady explained. 'But she only stayed with us for three days before she ran off. We brought her home from Norwich where we went on holiday. She was a stray wandering around the hotel car park. I am really glad she has a happy home now.' Norwich is 50 miles away.

A pity the cat did not stay in Norwich, I thought, but as long as she keeps out of my lounge I suppose I can tolerate her. I planned to keep her under observation.

AN IDEA IS BORN

Diana and Ruth met regularly for a chat and to ride out the ponies on the farm. One day Ruth asked Diana how her work with the cat charity was going. Diana replied that she was looking for an interesting way to promote the message of the importance of spaying and neutering cats. This would help to avoid the distress caused by unwanted kittens being born and male cats wandering off, getting lost and also suffering from diseases transmitted through fighting.

We cats are very good at reproducing: it is our plan for World domination over the dogs. One female cat is programmed to be able to give rise to around 45 kittens a year if her kittens have kittens at five months of age. Unfortunately, we have become so good at reproducing that there are not enough happy homes for all the kittens to find and many of them end up in very sad situations. I wanted to help Diana and Ruth do something about this.

I knew I had to help. I tried to tell them my ideas, but all that came out was a very loud and enthusiastic purr. This happens when I get excited. 'Purrrr, Purrrrr'.

They ignored me at first: they were engrossed in their discussions. So I tried again a little louder.

'She's really going for it today!' Diana was quick to comment.

'Eureka! I've got it' exclaimed Ruth 'a purring competition. That would attract the media's attention and get our message across. Let's organise a purring competition in Northampton. It does not matter if Smokey doesn't win, just as long as the radio runs with the story we will get the publicity for the Charity'.

'Brilliant' said Diana.

'Brilliant' I thought. 'But it does matter if I don't win. I am the top cat. I am Smokey the purring cat' A few calls later, and Ruth and Diana had set up a date with BBC Radio Northampton station so that I could demonstrate my loud purring skills on air.

The all-important day came and the three of us headed into town to the radio station head office. I felt rather nervous as I could tell something very exciting was about to happen. It had been decided not to host a competition on air but we would talk about the excellent work that Cats Protection did for us felines. My job was to add the sound effects of a happy cat.

We were shown to the vacant studio, so we could see John Griff, the presenter, through a window as he was making his broadcasts. We were told to wait in there until we could see a green light which would indicate that we may enter the studio and he would be ready for us. John was very friendly and very talkative. He told us to watch his eyes as this was how he would indicate to us when he wanted to speak to us by looking at us. I was feeling very scared now. My heart was pounding so much in my chest I thought that I would explode. The whole room seemed to hiss with electronic equipment. I was feeling very dizzy and very small. I panicked.

Ruth and Diana chatted very naturally, as though it was a perfectly normal day, but my purr stuck in my throat. I wanted to be out of there. When we returned to the original room and I saw my cat basket and pink blanket a feeling of relief swept all over me and the tension inside me was released in an explosion of purr. I was going home and I was happy.

Unknown to me a switch connecting the two studios was flicked and my loud purr was broadcast to the residents of Northampton. This was my first purr broadcast.

While I was purrforming at the radio station, some very unflattering pictures were taken of me. I looked rather like a limp puppet being held up to the microphone. I'm not surprised I did not purr well looking at these images.

CAT FACT

One female cat has the biological capacity to give birth to 420 kittens in her life time. Each of these kittens can also reproduce at five months of age and may have between three and seven kittens every four months. That can lead to a lot of cats and a population explosion. This is why it is very important to spay or neuter any cats which you do not plan to breed from.

The awful pictures were sent to the local newspaper, *The Northampton Chronicle & Echo* and thankfully, they agreed with me that the pictures were not flattering, and so they sent out a separate photographer the next day to photograph me.

I was much happier about this as the photographer obviously appreciated my beauty. Do I sound vain? It's just that being a cat I take a real pride in my appearance. I loved being the centre of attention, and so I purred, and I purred. Louise, the photographer, recorded my purr on her mobile telephone as she knew I sang so beautifully.

On Wednesday 16 February 2011, an article appeared in *The Northampton Chronicle & Echo* with a photograph of me sitting on my window sill with my owner, Ruth. I do not know why she has her hands over her ears, in the picture it looks rather silly as she would not be able to hear me purring. The story asked if 'Smokey had the loudest purr of any cat in Northamptonshire?'

In order to allow their readers to hear my wonderful purring tones the newspaper had arranged for my purr song to be placed on the internet on their web site. This is all very high tech stuff for me.

Apparently a lot of people clicked on their computer mouse and listened to my purr. One of these was from a media agency which was located some 50 miles to the east of Northampton. I was very impressed that my fame had spread so far.

My family were having their tea that evening when the telephone rang. I was annoyed as this would delay the serving of my dinner. I circled around Ruth's legs impatiently while she picked up the receiver. I wanted to remind her that I needed feeding, and my curiosity had got the better of me so I needed to eavesdrop on the conversation.

'We think the story of your loud purring cat has National interest and we wish to send a photographer with a decibel reader to the farm tomorrow to record your cat. How about tomorrow morning? It would be brilliant publicity for Cats Protection', the caller tempted Ruth.

For those fellow cats who do not know – a decibel reader is an instrument used to record the volume levels of sound waves as they travel through the air.

A totally bemused owner agreed, and everything was arranged. In my excitement at another photo opportunity I forgot that my meal was late in being served.

PICTURES & MORE

17 February 2011

The next day, my owner settled me on to the square padded pouffe, gave me a few biscuits and sprinkled catnip around me to drive me crazy with happiness (catnip is a herb which gives a wonderful smell and adored by many cats), while the photographer, Geoff, set up.

A strange-looking device like a plump padded plastic mouse was placed in front of me and Ruth started to stroke me in my favourite place. I started to relax, I loved the stroking and so I purred and I purred. The electronic mouse flickered and the numbers on the screen moved. The louder I purred the higher the numbers went. I could sense the excitement in the air and it sent a tingling through my body. I was the centre of attention and I loved it.

80 decibels, 85 decibels, 92.7 decibels, Ruth and Geoff, the photographer, recorded the figures. The numbers meant nothing to me but I could tell they were pleased.

The camera clicked and clicked. I was starting to tire of the electronic mouse game and I felt like a stretch and a yawn. I jumped down from my seat deciding to take a short break. I was immediately plonked back on the box and was told to 'sit and stay'. How rude! Do they think I am a delinquent dog without the power of independent thought!

A bribe of a few more biscuits quickly purrrsuaded me to remain and the photographer took not 10 but 100 variations of the same picture. I was relieved when the session was over and I could retire to grab a drink and a cat-nap on my cushion on the window sill.

The media agency called that evening to say that they were amazed by the high decibel readings which I had generated and maybe I should consider applying for the Guinness World Records record for the 'Loudest Purring Cat in the World'. This would be a new category that Guinness World Records had created and they were looking for an outstandingly loud purring cat to set the initial record. Well we had to try, didn't we!

THE NATIONAL PRESS

22 February 2011

On 22 February 2011 my world changed forever. My fame as a loud purrer was being written about in most of the British national newspapers. Articles appeared in *The Daily Telegraph, The Daily Mail, The Daily Mirror, The Star, The Sun, The Observer* and *The Times* to name but a few.

The newspapers were comparing my purr to a sound level which would be equivalent to a Boeing 747 coming in to land from a mile away, or lawn mower, vacuum cleaner and hairdryer. Ooops…maybe I should consider toning things down a little; I do not want to be considered anti-social.

Newspapers were spread all over the carpet in front of me, and Ruth and Amy were busy cutting out the articles to stick them in a red file. They were very excited.

The radio interviews came first before the television crews arrived. I developed the art of the live purr interview over the telephone. Ruth and I would be given a time to be sitting by the telephone awaiting a call for an interview on air with a radio station. Ruth would put the telephone receiver close to my mouth and I would sing happily to them while being

Ruth Adams and Smokey, the Guinness World Records record holder for the 'Loudest purring domestic cat'.

Image supplied by The Northampton Chronicle and Echo newspaper.

Buttercup the hen is wrapped in a towel.

Tilley, the goat enjoys the sandwiches and cakes.

Smokey attends the Pet Service at the local church.

The Veterinary ambulance with Mr Chris Heaton-Harris MP, Kay James veterinary nurse and Diana Johnson.

Smokey makes her first Guinness World Records record attempt.

Smokey eyes up a piece of bacon and purrs louder.

RION Sound level meter NA-28 .

Left to right are Diana Johnson, Chris Heaton-Harris MP, Kay James, Raymond Meadham and seated Ruth Adams and Smokey.

The second Guinness World Records record attempt for the loudest purring cat. Ray watches the decibel reader while reporters from the *Northampton Chronicle & Echo* newspaper watch and listen while Smokey purrs loudly.

Smokey makes a second attempt at the Guinness World Records record for the 'loudest purring domestic cat'.

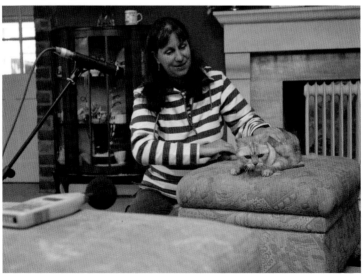

Smokey the cat was feline fine after recieving her official Guinness World Record for being the loudest purring domestic cat in the world. Owner Ruth Adams, from Pitsfod, near Northampton, and technicians from Northampton College, who recorded the successful attempt, were delighted with the result of almost 68 decibels.

Smokey the cat and owner Ruth Adams sign copies of the new book of Guinness World Records at Waterstones in Northampton. Smokey is now featured in the book for having the loudest recorded purr.

Smokey meets the reception staff at Town and Country Veterinary Centre open day in Market Harborough.

Smokey 'looks' at the atlas.

Smokey supervises work on her book.

Smokey meets a television company from the Ukraine.

This page and opposite: Anglia Television filmed Smokey's favourite window from the inside and out.

Puss Puss soon made herself at home in the stable yard.

Amy Adams (aged 11 years) and Smokey.

Ruth Adams pictured at her home in Pitsford with Smokey.
Image supplied by The Northampton Chronicle and Echo newspaper.

Smokey is interviewed by Natalie Verney for Heart FM radio.

Picture taken by Smokey's owner and sent to Guinness World Records. Shame about the wonky horizon! This picture taken by Ruth was used in the Guinness World Records book.

John Griff presenter of the afternoon show for BBC Radio Northampton with Smokey in the studio.

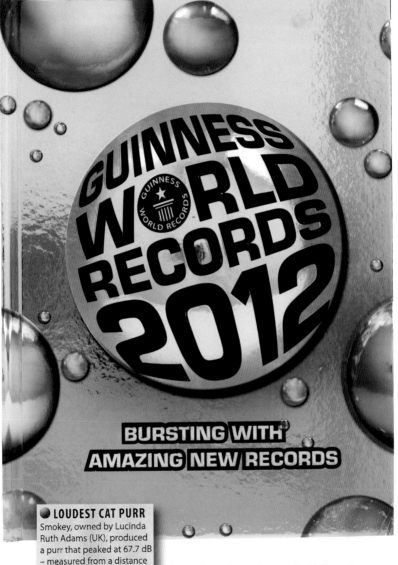

GUINNESS WORLD RECORDS 2012

BURSTING WITH AMAZING NEW RECORDS

● LOUDEST CAT PURR

Smokey, owned by Lucinda Ruth Adams (UK), produced a purr that peaked at 67.7 dB – measured from a distance of 1 m (3 ft 3 in) – the loudest by a domestic cat, on 25 March 2011. This purr-fect achievement took place at Spring Hill farm, Pitsford, Northampton, UK.

CERTIFICATE

The loudest purr by a domestic cat
is 67.7 dB (LA peak) and was
achieved by Smokey, owned
by Lucinda Ruth Adams (UK)
at Spring Hill farm,
in Pitsford, Northampton, UK,
on 25 March 2011

GUINNESS WORLD RECORDS LTD

stroked and fed tasty treats. I looked forward to these calls as I enjoyed the treats.

I purred to radio stations in Australia, America, Canada and the Gulf States as well as numerous stations around the United Kingdom, including Radio 5 Live, Heart, Northampton's Inspiration FM and BBC Radio stations in Birmingham, Warwick and Northampton. My story was also aired on BBC Radio 4, so now I really was serious news.

The telephone kept ringing with interested enquiries from other media outlets all over the world. Someone needs to tell the Australians that there is a time difference between the UK and their country.

Australia at this time was recovering from the worst devastating floods since 1974 when the Brisbane River burst its banks after very heavy rainfall. A large area of Queensland had been declared a disaster zone, with 15 people dead and at the time 61 people were missing. Around 15,000 properties were either destroyed or submerged in the muddy waters. Over 200,000 people were affected as homes were swept away like discarded match boxes.

Our interview was to follow a news article interviewing a gentleman about his experiences and eyewitness accounts of the floods. We were listening to the Australian broadcast live over the telephone and even though several months had passed since the disaster, the stories were no less harrowing. I could tell that Ruth was becoming unsettled by this as she stopped stroking me.

The man graphically described a lady clinging to the chimney on the roof of her house to avoid being swept away. The gentleman spoke of his agony at being unable to help. I wished we could have done something. I did not want to purr. How could I purr having heard such a distressing story?

The dramatic roof top drama finished and I was left unaware whether or not the story had a happy ending. The radio station then switched to an advertising commercial promoting the benefits of some special car tyres. I was not sure if they mentioned 'good in wet' conditions as one of their selling points! What am I doing here? I do not want to do this interview anymore, I thought. Then came the words… 'and now it's live now over to the United Kingdom for a very special guest for our show. Now listen carefully and tell us what this noise is?' The receiver was put to my mouth and I thought I'd better help Ruth out by purring for Australia. Ruth then chatted away and tried to sound jolly and enthusiastic about the fact that I could be the world's loudest purring cat. I knew she was not happy. A cat can tell, we can sense emotions.

The interview over, it probably only lasted about two minutes and the presenter had an off-air chat with us to thank us and reassure us that the story went down well. In difficult times sometimes a light-hearted story could help out by brightening spirits, she explained. We felt a lot better after that; however, we were still a little sad. When you watch these images on your television, they are somehow detached from you, but now we felt a connection. The story was real and not a fictional disaster movie.

Further interviews on the radio followed, including the BBC World Service. Somehow I suddenly felt the urge to purr with a new sophisticated more official purr, one with an English accent: I was now purring for England.

CAT FACT

Lions and Tigers can't purr properly. If they tried to purr it would sound more like a splutter; however, the big cats can roar which makes up for the inability to purr.

Purr-fect Smokey is feline fine

THIS cat may look absolutely purr-fect but 12-year-old Smokey is fast driving her Northamptonshire owners mad with her exceptionally loud miaow.

Ruth and Mark Adams, of Pitsford, find it impossible to hear the television or radio when their pedigree pet decides to express her contentment with the world, and struggle to maintain telephone conversations in which their pet seems determined to be the centre of attention.

Mrs Adams, whose family also owns two other cats and two dogs, said she believed Smokey had the loudest purr of any cat in Northamptonshire.

She said: "It's either adorable or annoying, depending on what mood you're in. It's very loud and you don't have to stroke her to start a purring session.

"I don't really know why she does it. It doesn't seem to bother her in any way. She's very happy and content, she's just very loud."

Smokey, a former rescue cat, is helping Northampton Cats Protection promote the importance of spaying or neutering animals to prevent unwanted litters.

Cats Protection is offering vouchers to help with the costs of such procedures. Call 08447 003251 or visit www.northampton.cats.org.uk

Northamptonshire Chronicle and Echo newspaper, Wednesday February 16, 2011.

I AM ON TV!

Three British film crews came over the next few days. These were Anglia TV, BBC Look East and the national morning television show *Daybreak*. Amy was very excited as she had been granted permission for a day off school to join in the filming.

The previous day had been a very busy one, as a mammoth clean of the house was underway. Tables were polished, windows cleaned, floors mopped and carpets vacuumed. The air was a mixture of polishes and air fresheners and 'Shake and Vac' – all fighting for supremacy. I can't decide if apple blossom or honey wax was the winner, but they both smelled awful. When you are a cat your nose is far more sophisticated than a mere human's nose. I coughed up two hairballs on the sofa.

When satisfied that there were no other possible ways to improve the lounge or half-decorated kitchen, Ruth went upstairs to try to decide the best clothes to wear for each interview.

Outfits were laid out and then put back in the wardrobe. As a cat I can't understand this obsession with a colour change. I'm silver and stripy grey today, and will wear the same stripy grey jump suit next week, and no-one has ever told me that I'm not in fashion. I do admit that sometimes my coat makes me look a little plump, but that really goes with my image of the contented purring cat.

Each television company that came to the farm sent a pair of people: an attractive young female presenter and in contrast, a more rugged sturdy camera man. The pretty female ladies were very relaxed and clearly appreciated my many talents, but the older film men were far more serious and less playful. I could sense they were agitated if I did not look at their camera at the exact moment they felt I should or if I shuffled across the carpet to check them out. I do not think they realised that I was in charge of the photo shoot and they were to move around me.

The cameras were huge, about four times my size. They were either placed on tripods or were carried rather clumsily on the camera man's shoulders. They looked very heavy.

My attention was focused on the hairy grey fluffy microphone on a pole which was always hovering over me. It reminded me of my distant cousin, Max, so I gave it a sniff to find out if he had met an untimely demise and been stuffed and stuck on a stick. Maybe that's what they do with cats who won't sit still for the cameraman. Fortunately it did not smell of a cat, so I think it was an imitation placed there to remind me to behave.

Camera crews like to practise their art, and try to film their star from a multitude of angles; these are called 'takes'. Sometimes I found them a little in my face, especially when they zoomed in for a close-up. I don't think they realise how intimidating a massive lens can be when it is pushed in to a cat's personal space. A few sharp hisses were required to remind them.

Although each rival film crew had planned separate ideas on how best to demonstrate my purring abilities, they all ended up producing similar news footage. This involved my purring loudly next to general household objects, such as a washing machine, food blender, vacuum cleaner and hairdryer. It was a kind of competition to see which were the loudest. Of course I won!

Perhaps my favourite television film crew came from a country called Ukraine. Ruth and I had to look at an atlas before they visited to familiarise ourselves with where on Earth the Ukraine was. For fellow cats that do not know, it's found next door to Russia.

The crew of two who turned up loved me instantly and the friendly female presenter scooped me up and gave me lots of cuddles. I appreciated this somewhat forward move as it made this crew seem more human than the other television companies.

I think the talking part of the interview may well have flowed a little easier for Ruth if she had been able to speak a little Russian, but purring is the same whatever language so I was able to help her out. I suggested halfway through the filming that it might be a good idea to adjourn to the garden for a different scene as I had a few duties of a personal nature which needed my attention. Once in the garden we played a little chase me hunting games, which I hoped they enjoyed, as the camera man followed me through the bushes and over the flower beds. I am still very agile even though I am 12 years old. When I eventually allowed them to catch me, we ended filming with some cute cuddle pictures next to the garage. It was a very fun day and I really enjoyed the jolly relaxed nature of the Ukraine people. Hello Ukraine, I like you.

Everything about America is larger than life; it is a very exuberant nation across the Atlantic Ocean. I have seen a lot of Americans on the television when Ruth and I watch movies together. Many films are set in the United States and there certainly are lots of things going on over there. They speak English with a rather strange accent, but then I am just a cat.

I had two American film crews turn up at the farm to film me. Thankfully they did not arrive on the same day, as they were fierce hissing rivals of each other, both competing to attract the greater viewer ratings.

First to arrive was ABC News, part of the Disney Corporation. I mention this as I have seen a lot of very good Disney films about fellow animals, which I have enjoyed watching. A Disney film always has a happy ending. They were filming for the morning News Programme *Good Morning America*, which is broadcast nationally over the whole of the United States. America is massive.

They arrived via a mini-bus and a crew of five descended on the farm house. Outnumbered, big time, I wanted to bolt for my cat flap. Diana, my friend from Cats Protection, had turned up as well to provide moral support and make the endless cups of coffee which we knew the Americans liked to drink.

Things were a little cramped in our lounge. Each of the Americans had a job allocated, so we had a producer, a presenter (who, Ruth and Diana agreed was rather good-looking), a camera man, a sound technician and a driver.

If I had not been so stressed out I would have been amazed to see them in action.

I am not sure how to describe the magic green oval shaped screen which exploded out of a bag. It sprung out of the holdall and unfolded into a wall of bright slime green cloth within seconds. Not a very fetching colour I thought, may be a pastel blue would be more suitable as a backdrop.

Ruth, following directions from the producer, placed me on a pouffe in front of the green wall and asked me to keep very still and purr loudly for 30 seconds. They are very precise these Americans. Apart from swishing my tail in a subtle protest, to which they were oblivious, I did as I was told.

They then had a strange obsession with our fireplace, and took several pictures of it without anyone standing in front of it. Maybe they do not have stone fireplaces in the States I thought. Next there followed lots of pictures of Ruth and I watching television together. I do enjoy competing with the television volume levels with my purr if I feel the programme needs revving up a little, or if I just feel like it.

Being a cat, I did not understand what they were doing, as the four hours of filming seemed so disjointed. Perhaps that's what happens when you put too many Americans in a room together, they can't agree from which angle to take the picture, I thought. I was totally bemused how this jigsaw of film takes was ever going to be pieced together.

I was so exhausted after the ABC film crew left. I had found it a very tiring day and I went to collapse behind the sofa. Was I really up to all the demands of being a celebrity cat? Maybe I had not really thought about the rigorous filming schedule I had agreed with Ruth to take on. I began to question my career path.

Two days later, it was the turn of NBC, the National Broadcasting Company from America, to do their filming. They were producing footage for the *Today* programme. By comparison to their rival's at ABC, they were far more casual and sent a mere crew of two people; a camera man and a producer. No presenter this time.

This seemed to be a relatively stress-free filming session and was all over very quickly. I purrformed my usual routine of singing along with household objects and they went away looking suitably impressed. I felt very pleased with myself. This time I had managed to satisfy the Americans in two hours. I was obviously getting better at this filming lark. I had a good stretch and jumped up on my window sill.

I was very excited to view the news footage as it would be going out the next morning. Both ABC and NBC wished to be first to air my story across the Atlantic so that they could claim a news scoop. I could hardly sleep that night.

Proverbs About Cats From Around The World
'In a cat's eye, all things belong to cats'
English proverb

'Happy owner, happy cat. Indifferent owner, reclusive cat'
Chinese proverb

'After dark all cats are leopards'
Native American proverb

'Happy is the home with at least one cat'
Italian proverb

'Cats, flies and women are ever at their toilets'
French proverb

'Beware of people who dislike cats'
Irish proverb

'An old cat will not learn to dance' Moroccan proverb

'The cat was created when the lion sneezed'
Arabian proverb

'When rats infest the palace a lame cat is better than the swiftest horse.'
Chinese proverb

THE WORLD GOES WRONG

12 March 2011

*'No matter how much cats fight, there always seems to
be plenty of kittens'*
Abraham Lincoln

During the night a colossal natural disaster happened in Japan. A
devastating earthquake shattered the northern half of the country: the
Earth's crust shook violently and buildings toppled like a stack of
dominos.

Worse was yet to happen as the raised Earth's surface under the sea
dislodged a large mass of sea water and sent a tidal surge cascading
over the already stricken country. The huge wall of water was called a
tsunami. The water travelled so quickly and with such force that escape
for all was virtually impossible and hundreds of people and animals
perished under the muddy mass of water and debris. Even when the
waters subsided there was further danger for the surviving residents of
the stricken area as several of the nuclear electricity-producing power
stations had been damaged and their dangerous contents of

radioactive waste risked leaking out. We watched the images of the destruction on our television hardly able to comprehend the scale of the problems that Japan was now facing. Satellite cameras beamed horrific images across the globe as the whole world watched and shuddered in disbelief. I felt very guilty that I had been purring yesterday. The images of Japan were harrowing. How can something naturally occurring be so destructive? I pondered.

The telephone rang and both of the two American television companies explained that they would be unable to feature Smokey at this time as scheduled, as they needed to concentrate on the developing situation in Japan. We totally understood. This was not a time to purr. For once I was silent.

The world was going wrong, but it was not only natural disasters which provided shocking headlines internationally. Suddenly I was addicted to watching the global news, as I was the only cat on the planet whose news story release depended on the correct global state of calm before my story of purring was deemed appropriate to be aired. The American film crews sent our news filming to the vault until the world felt better. A country called Libya also hit the global news with stories of its civil unrest and battles going on between its own civilians. The country was imploding and fighting internally and other nations were becoming interested in what was going on.

Being a cat this was impossible for me to comprehend, all I did know was, that with such unhappiness going on in the world it was not a good time to purr loudly. I opted to lay low and put my purring on mute. I have never told my family where my mute button is in case they over-use this facility.

THE POWER OF THE INTERNET

You may have thought that that was it – job done! Not so, due to the incredible power of the internet the story continued to spread around the world. Thousands of people began to follow Smokey's story on the internet, but not all were happy with hearing about it.

Several newspaper sites allowed people to post their comments. The majority of the comments left were very encouraging but a few people were not very happy and to show that I am writing a fair story I thought I should include a few of the negatives. Ruth became sad that we had upset so many people.

'Is this really news?'

'Must be a slow news day'.

'I have just wasted 12 seconds of my life listening to a clip on that cat' (and about two minutes thinking of how to respond!).

'My cat's louder'.

'Only loud if you turn up the volume'.

'Not a purr, respiratory disease, sounds like a bronchial infection. They need to see a vet'.

'That cat is calling someone, not purring'.

'I am not an easily frightened person, but I might need an underwear change if I heard something like that out on a dark night in an unfamiliar and wild area. In a house it's a different story, but you'd need a set of earplugs when it's hungry or affectionate.'

'I've heard cats in the neighbourhood louder than that.'

'Take a listen to Smokey for yourself and decide if you think this is the world's loudest cat – How could you possibly answer that question??? It's a recording, recorded at a certain level and played back at a certain level...could be softer than a feather falling or louder than an aircraft at take off...one things for sure, no audio-engineer involved in this article'.

'Ha-Ha, sounds like snoring, not purring'.

'Loudness depends on distance and is distorted if measured close up'.

'My girlfriend makes a noise like that'.

'I wonder if it is also the world's tastiest cat'. [How rude I thought].

Clearly it's impossible to please everyone, but it makes for a more interesting story to include them and hopefully I can repay the man who was annoyed he had wasted 12 seconds of his life by giving him 12 seconds of fame back in return.

Via the internet we were able to see that newspapers all around the world were covering the story of my loud purr. I really did feel International.

CAT FACTS ABOUT PURRING

There are two theories as to how a cat can purr. The first is that the cat has an extra set of false vocal cords in its throat which allow the cat to make a rumbling purr sound for hours without having to open its mouth.

The second theory suggests that the purr noise is created due to turbulence in the blood flow through the cat's chest and this noise is then amplified in the cat's skull.

Cats do not always purr because they are happy sometimes they purr because they are anxious and are requesting support. The purr is a plea for friendship. A cat may purr when it is pain.

A VERY IMPORTANT
E-MAIL

15 March 2011

In the meantime the information pack from Guinness World Records arrived via E-mail. We were very pleased. The initial excitement soon turned to shock. This was going to be a lot more complicated, than I, or Ruth ever imagined. It was easy to accidently claim that you were applying for a Guinness World Records record, but it was going to be virtually impossible and very expensive to prove it.

Ruth read, and re-read the multiple pages of the attached schedule, trying to get to grips with the technical jargon, and how on earth she could possibly comply with the very strict criteria for claim evidence which Guinness World Records were requiring. She cried.

'I am not sure how to deal with this or how to get out of this mess? What have I done?' she sobbed.

Guinness World Records offers three systems for would be applicants to prove their World Record Breaking claims.

The first option is a completely free service and is the option that the majority of applicants select. A decision is usually made within a few weeks of a claim being registered and all the evidence being received. This is truly remarkable considering the huge volume of applications that Guinness World Records receive every week.

For those who simply can't wait because they are so excited about the possibility of being a Guinness World Records record Holder then there is a more speedy 'fast track claim assessment' service. With this queue jumping 'fast track' system, provided that all the appropriate information and evidence is supplied, the appropriate Guinness World Records advisor will contact you within days to advise you with your application. There is a fee for this service which currently is around £400. These were the only two options which myself and Ruth could practically consider.

The third option which is way out of our league is for a 'personal adjudicator' to attend and witness a Guinness World Records record attempt. For those with a larger budget this is defiantly the best option. It often provides extra media interest and excellent photographic opportunities and you can have an instant decision and be awarded your certificate, if you are successful.

Ruth checked her purse and hand bag to see if she had the required £3,000–£5,000. She counted up and announced that we had £21.23 available to finance our Guinness World Records record attempt and so we opted for standard claim application. I suggested using the £21.23 to purchase some hammy, bacon treats for myself. But I did not mind waiting, the longer we waited the more tasty treats I would receive in my purr training sessions; take your time I thought.

I sat by Ruth on the desk by the computer and we examined the extensive details which Guinness World Records sent to us about proving our claims. These were as follows.

In brief (I am going to edit, as being a cat I do not read so well) any official Guinness World Records record attempt for the new category of 'loudest purring domestic cat' should satisfy, or include the following:

1) Must be carried out in front of official witnesses, which should include at least one public notary figure; suggestions included a doctor, lawyer, Justice of the Peace, police officer, Member of Parliament or ordained minister of a religion (apologies if I have not listed your profession). Also required would be a veterinary professional and another witness who should be a professional sound engineer with several years' experience. The three or more witnesses are to write 'official' witness statements. This all sounded very official.

2) The volume of my purring was to be recorded using a Category 1 sound decibel level reader, which supplies a data print-out. This is a very technical and expensive piece of equipment. The machine was to be calibrated to a set distance of 1 metre away from myself.

3) My record attempt is to take place outdoors with a background noise level not to exceed 20 decibels. This is because walls could reflect and amplify my purring, possibly making it appear louder. A back ground noise of 20 decibels is the same amount of noise you would hear if a pin dropped, or a few leaves rustled, or if someone gulped in disbelief.

4) The microphone should be positioned at 1.6 metres above the ground. The cat may sit on a chair [with a cushion I hoped].

5) The whole of the Guinness World Records record attempt should be videoed and a tape produced of not more than an hour [being already used to purring to camera this did not worry me at all].

6) High-quality photographs were to be taken. [So, no good my owner taking them then or they would not even be in focus!]

7) The attempt should allow full public access [this was a little scary as I do not always feel comfortable with strangers until I have sniffed them].

8) A purr level should have a peak of not less than 75 decibels at a distance of 1 metre away [this was going to be hard to deliver at a distance of 1 metre away].

OOPS! I thought. This is not going to be easy, especially when you have no budget (apart from £21.23 in Ruth's handbag which I wanted for my tasty treats) to carry out a Guinness World Records record attempt.

Ruth called several decibel meter hire companies to find out what was involved. I am not sure how much they cost to hire per day, but she cried again. This was clearly going to need some serious finance.

Ruth made several telephone calls asking for help in tracking down a suitable decibel reader, but unfortunately, the response of 'no help, not our sort of thing, but we wish you good luck' was given.

Luckily, ANV Measurement systems, distributor for RION the world's second largest manufacturer of sound and vibration readers was conveniently located at Milton Keynes, which was only 25 miles away from our home town. It's amazing what information you can find out in the comfort of your own home by doing some research on a computer.

They were very interested to talk to Ruth and myself about our difficulties with complying with the requirements requested by Guinness World Records. Ruth and I felt more confident now having knowledgeable advisors to explain the technical jargon to us.

They advised us that it would be very hard for anybody to satisfy these requirements, as to achieve a background noise of less than 20 decibels; I would need to be sitting on my chair three miles away from the nearest road in the middle of a field. The image of me as a scarecrow sprang to mind and I definitely did not want to purr. This did not sound cosy and I really am not the outdoor pursuits type. I am strictly a comfortable sofa girl.

I tried to picture an image of people hiking three miles carrying all the equipment, and my chair and cushion to a desolate place and then spending a few hours to set up, and it then being spoilt in the middle of our recording by a Boeing 747 flying overhead!

The scene of tranquillity would also require; no birds, no trees to rustle, no sheep to bleat, no cows to moo, absolutely no breeze and definitely no spectators chatting or chewing sweets. So we looked at our atlas and decided that there would be no such place in the United Kingdom.

When you walk outside you are often not aware of the background noise which surrounds you because you become accustomed to it being there. If you wander around the open countryside and especially around towns, life can be very noisy. We suddenly became tuned into different everyday noises.

Suddenly satisfying Guinness World Records' requirements had become more difficult than producing a mammoth purr in the first place.

Ruth contacted Guinness World Records via e-mails (this is their preferred method of communication with applicants) and suggested that using a soundproof room maybe a better option.

Guinness World Records receive on average 5,000 different claims for world records each week. Some of these claims are rejected on the grounds that they are dangerous, or would be cruel to my fellow animals. A World Record also needs to be based on fact and not opinion. Out of the 5,000 claims a week received, over 75 per cent are rejected; the remaining 25 per cent (1,250) are put forward for consideration as potential Guinness World Records record.

Thankfully Guinness World Records listened to our comments and a few days later a new set of guidelines arrived via e-mail. They were happy with the suggestion of using a soundproof room or studio. I was very glad that Guinness World Records were cat friendly and had adjusted the guidelines for the new category.

We contacted the local BBC Radio Station again to ask if we could possibly use one of their studios.

Unfortunately, they replied that their studios had a lot of hissing electrical equipment in the rooms and so were not silent, but they recommended, that we contact Northampton College as they had a Music Department.

Ruth rang the college, excited that she now felt that we were making some progress. Unfortunately, the receptionist thought that the call about a loud purring cat must be a student prank and she took a lot of convincing before she would really believe otherwise.

Our call was diverted to the Department of Music and a gentleman named Ray Meadham answered the telephone; Ray was curriculum manager for this department. Ruth repeated her plea for help, with me adding some very excellent backing vocals of vibrating purr. Ray was suitably impressed and offered to help us out with our Guinness World Records record attempt. We arranged a time for me and my cat basket to visit the college's sound booths for a purr practice and to checkout my decibel levels.

A LIVE SATELLITE INTERVIEW

20 March 2011

It was NBC News who contacted us first after a few weeks since their filming and said that they now wished to continue with the story of the Loud Purring Cat. They had already done two hours of filming but, they decided that as this was a news programme, it would make the story more alive and current if they organised a live satellite link with America.

This was a very scary proposition as NBC broadcasts to over five million viewers across America (according to the computer, on the 11 April 2011 NBC had 5,662,000 viewers). This means that you could make a complete idiot of yourself in front of a lot of potential viewers. This was going to be my biggest purrrformance yet.

The blue satellite van arrived at the farm at 9.30am on Sunday 20 March and we were scheduled to go live to America at 12.30pm, UK time. Due to differences in time between America and Britain, our lunchtime is their breakfast and the show was scheduled to air early morning in America.

The two satellite technicians spent three hours organising the links and rearranging the furniture in the living room. We had various practice shots, and I was rapidly beginning to tire of being endlessly moved around like a rag doll. If a cat is comfortable and purring loudly, that means do not move. Do not these guys understand cat talk? I was totally hissed off with them by the time it came to go live on air and I was feeling sick from over-indulging in the ham bribe.

I hissed and scratched and swore. I had decided I was definitely not going to purr. The technician was on the telephone trying to explain to his bosses why the loudest purring cat was now growling. A bit of emergency rescheduling was done and we were moved to a later slot in the programme to allow myself a little more time to compose myself and regain my purr.

An earpiece was fitted to my owner so that she could hear the show live in the American studio. I could feel her heartbeat pounding even though I was sitting on her knee. She was stressing me out even more. I could smell her fear and feel her tension. She was told that the American News anchor, Lester, would ask her a few questions via the earpiece and she was to always look at the camera and not down at the cat.

This was not a relaxing environment for purring and I hissed even louder. Ruth's stroking hand now stopped stroking and fastened firmly around my middle. I wanted out of here and nothing was going to stop me and so I dug my claws deep in to Ruth's lap just at the moment that she was saying 'Yes she's always purring she is one happy cat'.

I just loved the irony. This was not one of my better filming days.

Ruth found it very difficult while carrying out the interview. She had to pretend I was a happy cat and keep smiling, while we were having a mini battle on her lap. Ruth was also not expecting that there would be so much of a time delay between questions asked and answered as they were beamed up to the satellite and across the Atlantic Ocean. We both wanted out of there. I called 'time out', but I don't think they heard.

Ruth did not sleep well that night as she was convinced that she had just suffered international humiliation in front of millions in America. She was very sad. She said she 'was a doughnut'. Unfortunately our computer at home was having a 'can't do' sort of day and so we were unable to view the footage on-line until the next day when a neighbour arrived with her lap top computer.

Thanks to live on-air editing, bits of my previous purring footage was mixed with Ruth's interview and so our reputations of happy purring types was retained thankfully. Well done on-air editing team – we salute you.

It was the following day that ABC Television aired their footage on the *Good Morning America* show (which, according to my figures reached 4,812,000 viewers on 11 April 2011). Ruth and I were very relieved when we saw the show. They had very cleverly pieced together all the unrelated bits of filming and created a really funny news story. We loved it and now we understood; they had been working on a cunning plan all along.

The vile green coloured screen was not visible at all, in fact, completely the opposite – it was there to make things invisible and enabled them to superimpose my image in front of the fireplace, with which they had been so obsessed. They then added the presenter (good-looking), an aeroplane, a large car and a washing machine. The story then switched to the television scene and they demonstrated my art of purring over film clips. I loved the purring over Clint Eastwood '…come on punk make my…purrrr, purrrr' I loved it, brilliant and highly amusing. I award them my gold star for effort.

NORTHAMPTON COLLEGE

15 March 2011

On Tuesday 15 March, I was placed in my wicker cat basket and we had an excursion to Northampton College to meet Ray, the curriculum manager for their music department. Ruth was very excited. The college was undergoing an extensive rebuilding programme and was a hive of activity with the builders. Ray had arranged to meet us at the reception before taking us to the temporary home of the sound studios. He greeted us with a friendly smile and happy eyes.

He looked like a professional and efficient type of person and did not appear to be phased by the fact I was a cat. Ray introduced us to his technician who was waiting to greet us by the door of the recording studio. He was a younger person with wild, curly hair, he was somewhat bemused at seeing me.

I was not used to leaving my home and I felt very uneasy about my new surroundings. We entered a small square room which contained nothing but one blue padded chair in the middle and a microphone on a stand. Facing the chair was a large window beyond which the sound mixing desk could be seen.

My room reminded me of the interrogation cells I had seen so many times in the movies. It was not cosy, I could see no cat biscuits and I wanted to go home. I was nervous so I bolted towards the door, which I discovered was closed and possessed no cat flap, so then I circled round at speed before shooting straight back into the security of my cat basket for my ride home. The idea of purring never entered my head, this was a serious situation and I needed to escape.

'I don't think this is working, she is not very relaxed. I think it would be better if we brought the sound recording equipment to Smokey's home' suggested Ray. He is obviously used to dealing with the very talented highly strung artistic emotional types and knows how to keep us calm I thought.

'She does purr honestly' said Ruth not quite understanding why I had not delivered my loud purr on demand.

'Recording artists all have to be comfortable for them to purrform at their best'. He was trying to sound reassuring. I agree, I hissed from my cat basket – take me home.

The following week, Ray arrived at the farm with a collection of technical-looking equipment and lots of electrical wires. I felt a little guilty about my reluctance to purr the last time we had met, so rumbled a few notes or two from my purr box. We did a few practice purrs to check my levels at a distance of one metre away. He was suitably impressed, and agreed that we should attempt to set a Guinness World Records record for the 'Loudest Purring Domestic Cat.'

THE BIG DAY –
25 MARCH 2011

Another day for a big spring clean of the house, with more over-bearing smells of honey wax and apple blossom.

The furniture in the lounge was organised to allow maximum space around me, to keep the witnessing audience out of my face while I purred. Ruth arranged flowers, laid out all the Guinness World Records documents and press cuttings for the inspection by our witnesses. Refreshments were placed on the coffee table. Ruth did everything that she could possibly do to prepare, and then she did them all again to make sure nothing could go wrong. The rest was going to be down to me. The witnesses arrived and an invisible electricity of anticipation filled the air. This was going to be our big day and the world was waiting to hear the result.

Ray arrived punctually and settled himself on the edge of the sofa and placed the all-important decibel reader at the edge of the pouffe in front of my chair, at the required set distance of one metre away. All of our witnesses were told that they were to make no noise during the Guinness World Records record attempt, and they were to make a note of everything.

I can't say exactly when we started, because we didn't have a countdown or declaration of 'under starters orders and they are off,' but we started. I knew my job, look straight ahead and purr very loudly. We had been practising so hard for weeks prior to this day and nothing was going to stop me now. I tucked into a feast of ham and bacon to get myself in the happy mood and sang my heart out.

Ruth was not sure how many official witnesses Guinness World Records required and so she arranged for four witnesses plus Ray, our sound expert. Diana was present to represent Cats Protection and Kay, a veterinary nurse (with accompanying ambulance) from Abington vets attended to ensure the that I was not put under any undue stress during my bid. In charge of pictures was Alisdair from Digital-Nomad photography. Alisdair is also a British Airways captain. This proved useful for the comparison with Boeing 747 airplanes. To represent the human public and as our 'public notary figure' we asked the local MP along Mr Chris Heaton-Harris. That day we all felt like MP's – Member of Purrers!

All I needed to do now was purr very loudly. Ruth started to stroke me and so I revved up the purr a few notches and made it up to 69 decibels. I could see via the sign language that I needed to go higher. I was going to have to dig deep into my rib cage to find that extra blast of purr required. I arched my back straining to push out the last bit of purr left in me and I reached 73 decibels. That was it, I could do no more and my purring was all dried up. I had nothing left to give them.

The decision was made mutually by the group, not to try again, as I really had purred outstandingly already, 73 decibels represented a purring level 16 times louder than the average cat's purr. That would be like a horse galloping at 640 miles per hour instead of 40 miles per hour or a human sprinter doing the 100 metres in less than a second. Sixteen times better than normal, had to set a Guinness World Records record, we hoped.

This was all about establishing a level high enough for Guinness World Records to consider that Smokey could start the 'loudest purring cat' category. Although there may have been previous applicants, the purr levels achieved had not been exceptional enough to warrant being awarded the title. My purr having peaked at 73 decibels surely had to be a world-setting record, even though they had asked for 75 decibels.

We reported back to the publicity officer at Northampton College, who agreed to inform the Press Agency about our record attempt. The press release was immediately picked up Internationally and received coverage all over the globe.

The details, video, photographs and witness statements were all packaged up and sent off to Guinness World Records Towers in London for verification. The only thing left outstanding was to obtain the decibel print-out from the sound metre which the hire company said that they would organise when they found the suitable cable to connect it to their computer.

Now all we had to do was to have a frustrating wait for an answer. We were all satisfied that we had given it our very best shot.

In response to the immense international interest in my loud purring story, my owner organised with a friend, Ryan Wakeman, to set up a website so we could inform everyone about our progress with the Guinness World Records record attempt. I had my own website now. I felt very important.

www.smokeythepurringcat.com

THE HOUSESITTER
AND HOLIDAYS

Time had come for the Adams family (single 'd' in Adams, not to be confused with 'Addams' family from the horror series on television) to go away on their holiday's. I was very sad to watch them as they prepared to leave. They rushed around the house in a frenzy and I felt agitated and left out. I hated being separated from them. Margaret a close family friend was moving in to the house to keep me company but I did not want them to leave.

Puss Puss was taken to a local cattery for her holidays, so that she would not jump in the back of any visiting Lorries or leave any paw prints on the cars in the neighbouring office park. Both of these habits have caused a few problems in the past. I did not go with Ruth and the children to the cattery as it would bring back too many painful memories of my own time in captivity and so I let the family say the 'goodbyes' and 'see you soons'.

The cattery where Puss Puss was going for her holiday also provided a fostering service for Cats Protection and the children were very excited to tell me all about a female cat and kittens which were in their care.

The story goes a bit like this. A 'well-meaning' owner had placed a plastic flea repellent collar around her cat's neck but had fastened it too tightly. The female cat had had a good scratch and managed to get her front paw stuck inside the collar as she was trying to release it. The poor cat was unable to get her leg out or limp back home because she was on a hunting expedition some distance away from her home.

For six months neighbours in the area reported seeing a cat hobbling around on three legs but they were unable to get close to the cat to offer assistance. A rather frisky tom cat, however, was able to get close to her but he was not interested in giving her any assistance. He had other ideas and the cat soon found she was pregnant, as well as crippled.

Eventually she was so hungry and tired that she gave up the will to live and collapsed, fortunately in the garden of a cat lover who immediately picked her up and contacted Cats Protection. Forty-five minutes later, thanks to the very speedy action of the Cats Protection field worker, the cat was on the operating table receiving very urgent veterinary treatment and was released from the collar which had embedded itself into her flesh.

The cat needed an operation to stitch up her injuries, but because she was only about a week away from giving birth the vet was unable to operate until after she had had her kittens.

The good news is that Tasha, that's the name she has been given, gave birth to four healthy kittens and has now received attention to the injury on her neck. I hear that Tasha and her kittens are now doing well and all have new homes arranged.

The moral of the story is please fit snap-off collars to your cat to save anything similar happening as it did to Tasha.

Cat bids to break record

Ruth Adams with Smokey yesterday   MNCE-27-04-11-GM006

Smokey, it's got to be... purrfect

SMOKEY the pedigree rescue cat, famous for her loud miaow, may have set a new world record thanks to a top purr-formance.

The 12-year-old British short-hair was encouraged to purr in front of recording equipment yesterday by her owner Ruth Adams at her Pitsford home.

Ruth stroked, brushed and tickled Smokey under her chin and even fed her bacon and ham, to get her feline in the mood.

The data is now on its way to the Guinness World Record organisation, with the pair anxiously waiting to find out if judges will accept Smokey's effort.

Sound engineers from Northampton College marked a peak of 62 decibels in Smokey's purr, recorded from one metre away for clarity.

But once the distance has been factored in to the results, they believe it could be up in the 70s, enough to give Smokey the title.

Ruth became Smokey's eighth owner when she collected her from NANNA Animal Rescue three years ago.

By Emma Clark
Chronicle Reporter
emma.clark@northantsnews.co.uk

Ruth, who was supported by the Cat Protection Agency in the attempt, said: "She has always been very loud, always interrupting the television.

"She's just a very loud, happy cat, we fell in love with her straight away.

"We can't believe the attention she has received. We thought that maybe she was the loudest cat in Northampton but now it has gone worldwide.

"I'm a bit nervous about it, because I don't think this was her loudest purr. You never know what's going to happen when you're relying on an animal.

"But I really hope she has set the record. It will be very exciting."

Her pet cat has made headlines as far away as Australia, America and even Ukraine with the unusually loud sound she emits when tickled behind the ear.

For more information about Smokey, visit her website www.smokeythepurringcat.com

Northamptonshire Chronicle and Echo newspaper, Thursday April 28, 2011.

TROUBLE IN PARADISE

Digression over, and back to my story. The family left for their holidays leaving me in charge of the human house sitter, Margaret, and all of the animals on the farm. As the family were nearing the end of their vacation on 22 April, they received a call from our Guinness World Records claims adviser, asking for the missing data print-out sheet. This was not good news. This was a total bombshell.

'We need your data print-out by the close of business today or we will be unable to consider you for inclusion in the Guinness World Records book as it is going to the printers today.'

My Guinness World Records record bid was now in serious jeopardy and because of the time zone differences between Ruth's holiday destination and England; she was five hours behind UK time. This meant that she only had two hours to organise the delivery of a data print-out to London 4,000 miles away, and she did not have any telephone numbers of her witnesses with her.

Disaster.

Frantic telephone calls and e-mails to friends followed to try to locate Ray and the missing data print-out. Ruth rang the Northampton College but because of 'data protection' they would not release Ray's telephone number.

Diana pleaded with Guinness World Records for a time extension as it was impossible for Ruth being out of the country to locate the missing decibel print-out. All our efforts of proving that I truly was the Loudest Purring were collapsing.

Eventually Guinness World Records agreed with Diana's request to grant a one week extension to the deadline until the 5 May. They said that they would be hoping to include me in the 'stop press' section at the end of their very famous book.

We simply had to make the deadline for that book. We had all put in so much effort.

The clock was ticking. Can you believe it? I've achieved all the requirements for a Guinness World Records record, made countless television and radio performances, been all over the International press and achieved a purr 16 times louder than a normal cat at a calibrated distance of one metre away and I won't make it in to the famous book because a data cable was missing. I am HISSING MAD. I feel like the race horse who won the Grand National only for it to be voided because of a false start.

Where in the world was Ray and the missing data print-out? The answer to that was on an aeroplane also heading off on his holidays. Suddenly a bad situation was getting worse.

Ray was also shocked and equally as devastated as we were that the hire company had not done as they had promised and forwarded the data print-out to Guinness World Records. He had been assured that they would sort it out and had been pulling his hair out at the fact that they had so far not been able to produce a print-out as they had promised. Ruth agreed to communicate via e-mail when his plane landed. It had never been considered by Ruth or me that the data print-out would be an issue.

We had a deadline of just over a week. Ruth flew back to the UK on Sunday 24 April and Ray from somewhere else in the world was returning on the Tuesday. The data print-out had to be in London for Wednesday 4 May. As it was the Royal Wedding in Britain that week there were three bank holidays between these dates. This was going to require immediate and excellent co-ordinating. The reluctant, but only possible decision was made to redo the whole trial, with a different decibel reader, which would be guaranteed to produce the required print-out. There could be no room for error this time; a reliable machine was essential.

A Selection of the E-mails Sent

Subject: Re: The missing decibel print out
To: Ruth
From: Ray
Date: Friday, 22 Apr 2011, 09.01am
I have contacted one of my technicians and he has been desperately trying to get access to the machine used as we borrowed it. The people we borrowed it from did not have the cable to gain the print out. We have

been waiting for them to obtain this and supply the print out. My tech has been trying to get the machine and a print-out but we fear they are unable to provide the print out. I am sorry we are still trying. The witnesses did have access to view the meter during the recording and saw the 73 decibel reading. I will do my best to get the reading but assure you with the video and audio recordings were all taken within a metre of Smokey the measurements were accurate. I will chase up my tech and see what is happening. Ray

Subject: Re: The missing decibel print out
To: Ruth
From: Ray
Date: Friday, 22 Apr 2011, 11.10 am
Hi Ruth, I did send Guinness World Records a copy of the letter I sent to you on the 1st April and they have confirmed receipt. I will continue to chase up my team with regards to the print-out. I am Happy to do another session. I am away until Tuesday and will touch base then. Ray

Subject: Re: Smokey the second Purring trial
To: Friend Maureen
From: Ruth
Date: Friday, 22 Apr 2011, 12.17pm
Oh dear this does not sound good news. What have I done to upset the man in the sky? How can you set a Guinness World Records record but lose it because you do not have the cable plugged in. This is classic comedy, but excellent news for my book. This is going to turn in to a thriller! Ruth

Subject: Re: Smokey the second Purring trial

To: Ruth,

From: Ray,

Date: Saturday, 23 April 2011, 10.32am

I am still away. Could do wed morning or between 5 till 6pm on wed. I will leave a message for my tech to get equipment together. No students, around to film or photograph as college not back until Tuesday in May. I come back Tuesday. Ray

Subject: Re: Smokey the second Purring trial

To: Ray

From: Ruth

Date: Saurdayt, 23 Apr 2011, 11:13am

Hi Ray, I have heard from Diana and she is keen to do as second trial as well. She knows 2 police officers who may be able to be our official public notary figure. They work shifts so we will need to let them know what time and day. We could do the Thursday if this would give you more time to organise getting the equipment through the College, as otherwise it's a bit rushed for you. As long as we can get all the print out and statements done before the weekend, all would be fine.

Very exciting we are back on track. Really appreciate the second opportunity at the Guinness World Records record.

Could you let me know which day would be better so I can start organising witnesses etc.

Looking forward to hearing from you soon. I fly back tonight so will be back in UK Sunday morning and home at lunch time. Ruth

Subject: Re: Smokey the second Purring trial

To: Ray

From: Ruth

Date: Saturday, 23 Apr 2011, 13:26pm

Hi Ray,

Hope all is nice and sunny on your holiday. I am heading home today so mixed feelings as always homesick when away but I do enjoy holidays at the same time.

Brilliant about doing another trial, Wednesday 27th April it is then. I hate giving up in defeat I am always hopelessly optimistic and positive.

We will go for Wednesday morning then as 5-6 in the afternoon seems a bit tight to set up equipment and test all is working.

I will organise the video and photographer. I will let Diana know. Any problems can you ask your tech guy to call me so I can organise anything to help. I am not very technical but good at Googling and telephone calls. Many thanks.

Sorry to trouble you on holiday I just had a scary deadline to meet. Ruth

Subject: Re: A 2nd World Record Trial

To: Ray

From: Ruth

Date: Sunday 24th April

Hi Ray, I made it back to the UK but feeling totally jet lagged and on a different planet.

I am busy organising photographer, video and witnesses for Wednesday 27th April 2011.

I have informed Guinness World Records we are doing a retrial to get them a suitable Decibel print-out for use from a category 1 reader. Will be a bit more relaxed than previously as dare not ask MP and veterinary surgery again! It was embarrassing enough asking the photographer again. Will give it my best shot at organising what I can; it's a bit difficult with the Bank Holidays.

Thanks again for allowing us another attempt. I will have cat in training again tomorrow.

Enjoy your holiday.

Best wishes, Ruth

Subject: Re: A 2nd Guinness World Records record trail and I am home.

To: Diana

From: Ruth

Date: Sunday 24th April

Hi, Diana, I am now back in the UK. Ray is flying back to the UK on Tuesday. Wednesday seemed best option as we need to collate everything on Thursday to post. I need to source a photographer and video man. Ruth

Subject: Re: Smokey the second Purring trial

To: Ruth

From: Ray

Date: Tuesday, 26 Apr 2011 08:44am

I am collecting a different decibel machine from the firm in Milton Keynes rather than the one we used last time ta Ray

Ruth was going to have to organise a second Guinness World Records record trial while 4,000 miles from home. Looking at the diary the only option appeared to be to go for Wednesday 27th April. This would give enough time to collect the witness statements and pictures and post them to London on time for the deadline the following week. Ray agreed to help out and organise another decibel print-out recording. Both Ruth and Ray launched a two-pronged emergency plea for help to ANV Sound Measurement Systems of Milton Keynes. Why did we not use them the first time round? Which, as always, appears an easy question in hindsight. Could they supply us with a high quality reader which could produce a data print-out? The answer was 'YES! They would be delighted to help.'

Brilliant.

As time was so pressing, Ruth made a second emergency 'help needed' plea to Northamptonshire Newspapers, publisher of several local newspapers including the *Northampton Chronicle and Echo.* Could they help out by witnessing, videoing and supplying photographs for Smokey's Second Guinness World Records record bid?

'YES!' was the answer, they jumped at the chance at a world exclusive story!

Also ready to help out were Diana, from Cats Protection and Alisdair from Digital-Nomad photography.

Unfortunately, Kay and Chris because of the very short notice had other commitments for that day, but were devastated to hear of our difficulties. They wished us good luck a second time around.

A SECOND GUINNESS WORLD RECORDS RECORD BID

27 April 2011

I was very glad when my family returned home as I had missed them. They looked exhausted when they piled through the door and they had turned a funny colour a sort of blotchy red and brown. I purred with enthusiasm to see them. I really do not understand this desire to travel. It makes me very uneasy in case they forget to come back. The cases were unpacked and the washing machine rammed full of the contents from the cases. Life was getting back to normal.

Ruth and the children made a big fuss of me. I think they had missed me as well. But where was my present? The dogs were equally excited that we were all reunited. The family collected Puss Puss from the cattery. That part of normal I was a little bit jealous about.

After a night flight the family went into hibernation for the rest of the day, which was very frustrating because I needed attention and fuss.

The following day was the Monday bank holiday and for my family it was a mixture of catching up on all the household chores, grocery shopping and finalising my second Guinness World Records record trial on the Wednesday.

The big day came around again and time for more honey wax and apple blossom spray and fiddling around with the layout of furniture in the lounge. Again flowers arranged; documents and clippings laid out and snacks for the humans temptingly displayed on the coffee table. The chocolate brownie mini bites were a big success.

I knew what I had to do, but I was seething with rage at having to go through this whole ritual again. I was so cross I could not bring myself to take any interest in my pre-purr bribes of ham and bacon. I just wanted to get the session over and done with and retire to my favourite window sill for an afternoon nap.

Northamptonshire Newspapers sent a team of four people, a reporter, a photographer, a video man and an extra person as an observing witness. I knew I had better put on a good purrformance. Alisdair, the original photographer was also present and both photographers and video man set to work straight away to capture images of all the very technical looking equipment and myself in order to provide pictorial evidence for Guinness World Records.

The centre of attention this time was not me, but the RION NA-28 Decibel reader which was positioned one metre away on the end of the pouffe aimed towards myself. Ray checked, rechecked, and checked again, and the thumbs up ready to go signal was given.

This time everything had to work – there would be no more chances. I had the weight of the world's expectancy on my shoulders. I took a deep breath, closing my eyes so as to concentrate and to shield them from the glaring lights of the camera flashes. Let's go ready to rumble I thought, and I purred my paws off.

A peak reading of 67.7 decibels was reached. Not quite as good as before. I was disappointed with myself, but felt I had nothing left to give and so we all decided to rest there. 67.7 decibels was still 14 times louder than the average cat's purr.

The room emptied and now I could relax. I made my way into the other room to snuggle into my cushion on the window sill. I needed a wash, to freshen up. I wanted some me time, time alone. I placed the imaginary 'do not disturb' notice next to me and went to sleep.

ANV Sound Measurement systems e-mailed their report and data print-out across to Ruth's computer on the same day as the trial. In fact, their report arrived before even the first witness statement had been collected.

The next day the witness statements from Ray, Diana and Alisdair arrived and Ruth rewrote her accompanying letter. Ruth went to the offices of the newspaper to pick up the photographs and statements but only a CD disc of the video footage was ready to take away. So still remaining on the wanted list was the photographs, and witness statements from the *Chronicle & Echo* newspaper.

A ROYAL WEDDING

29 April 2011

Today Friday 29 April we were going to do absolutely nothing towards our Guinness World Records record attempt. Today was totally devoted to the Royal Wedding and nothing else in the world mattered.

England was very excited. The British people had been building up to this big day for months. The world's media had descended on the capital city of London as the Queen's grandson and second in line for the British throne, Prince William, was to marry his university sweetheart, Kate Middleton. It was going to be an incredible day of national pride and celebration.

The streets of the city were heaving with visitors trying to catch a glimpse of the happy couple and the royal procession. Everything was timed and delivered to perfection. Even all the Queen's horses did not put a hoof wrong. The soldiers looked splendid; every part of their official uniform was immaculately clean and polished. The royal carriages were stunning and looked like they belonged in a fairy tale. It was a truly splendid day and the whole world agreed. I watched the television from my window sill with fascination, how could so many people fit into such a small space?

Noisy moggy Smokey aims for a place in the record books

Purr-fect puss may be loudest in world

By John Harrison
Chronicle Reporter
john.harrison@northantsnews.co.uk

A PURR-TICULARLY noisy pussy cat has made an official bid to be declared the loudest feline in the world after Guinness World Record experts recorded her thunderous meow.

The owners of 12-year-old Smokey claim the moggy's ear-splitting purr is noisier than a lawn mower, a hair dryer and even a Boeing 747 coming in to land.

And having made headlines as far away as Australia, America and even Ukraine with the unusual sound she emits when tickled behind the ear, Smokey has now made an official attempt to purr her way into the record books.

On Friday, Northampton College set up an official world record attempt at Smokey's home, in Pitsford, using specialist sound equipment to record her. Smokey's ear-piercing purr was recorded at an extraordinary 73 decibels, 16 times louder than the average cat. Her owner, Ruth Adams, is now waiting to find out if Guinness will officially declare her the loudest purrer in the world.

She said: "Guinness has very strict criteria and the college has been very helpful in supplying the specialist recording equipment needed to measure Smokey's purr and for arranging the official witnesses.

"Smokey is actually quite camera shy so I was very conscious not to upset

her during the record attempt so we kept it all very calm and low key. We are very grateful to the college for stepping in to help us attempt the record and now just have to wait patiently to hear the final verdict."

Ray Meadham, from Northampton College, added: "You don't get asked to help out with a world record attempt every day so of course we jumped at the chance. We had a few test sessions at the college's studios before deciding to make the attempt in Smok-

Ruth Adams sets up some of the recording equipment used to see if Smokey the cat could purr her way into the record books for the loudest purr   *Submitted pictures*

ey's home environment where she felt more at ease and would perform at her best.

"The recording equipment we used to record Smokey's purr included a Rode microphone, Logic music software and a category 1 sound meter which measures decibels – it's the same equipment music professionals use. Luckily, Smokey was on top form and rose to the challenge."

To read more about Smokey's challenge visit www.smokeythepurringcat.com.

Northamptonshire Chronicle and Echo newspaper, Wednesday March 30, 2011

NOTHING GOES TO PLAN

We should have learned by now that we have no control over circumstances around us. All we needed was the witness statements and images from the newspaper. Ruth did not like to telephone the newspaper on Royal Wedding day as she knew that they would be busy.

Later on that Friday evening, Northampton proved to be the scene for the brutal murder of four members of a family by an unknown assailant. The police were hoping to trace a former business contact of the family to see if he could help with their enquiries. This was an unprecedented situation for the town of Northampton. Understandably all the local press were scheduling their efforts in trying to assist and report any developments in the story. Northampton was not used to being the centre of murder enquiries.

Normally this would have no connection at all to a purring cat story but for the fact that when Ruth rang the newspaper's office on the 2 May bank holiday Monday to ask for the urgent receipt of the pictures of the cat and witness statements she was told 'we have other priorities at the moment'. Ruth totally understood, but Guinness

World Records still required the images and all the evidence by 5pm on the Wednesday. Ruth did not feel she could call the newspaper back that day.

The images which Alisdair had taken had satisfied Guinness World Records that we had complied with their claim specifications, but what they were also looking for now, was a close-up more cuddly type of picture for inclusion in the 'famous book' and they wished to have a choice of more images.

Ruth remembered that a journalist had taken some excellent images of me when the story of my loud purr was first introduced to the press. The pictures were brilliant and would be just the high quality images that Guinness World Records would like to use for inclusion in their book. Ruth called the photographer to enquire if he could send the photograph he had taken of me to Guinness World Records for inclusion in their book but unfortunately the call was taken by an answer phone. Ruth left a message but knew that time was pressing as we only had just over 24 hours to supply our image for Guinness World Records. Unable at the time to obtain consent from the photographer for permission to use the image, Ruth knew she needed another plan. The picture editor was waiting. It was now 3pm on Tuesday and Ruth had until 5pm the next day to get all the proof and pictures to London.

There is a saying which goes 'if you want a job doing well, then do it yourself' and running out of options for getting this high-quality photograph to Guinness World Records in time, Ruth grabbed her camera and I joined her in the garden for an impromptu photo shoot. We took around 20 different pictures of me walking across the lawn and Ruth selected a couple and sent them across to their office in London.

Ruth called the local *Northampton Chronicle & Echo* newspaper again, trying not to sound desperate, as even though she felt it, she could hardly sound it without appearing insensitive to the victims of the murders in the town. The press were busy with important matters. Fortunately this time the telephone call was answered by David, the gentleman who actually took the video of the Guinness World Records record attempt – success.

'We'll get on to it' was the reply. That evening as if by magic a witness statement from David arrived and Helen from the newspaper sent through a collection of images which they had taken. The pictures looked very good. This was fantastic news everything was finally slotting in to place.

The pictures were e-mailed across to the Guinness World Records claim manager. However, the computer format of David's witness statement meant that Ruth was unable to send it across to Guinness World Records. This minor hiccup was solved and the last remaining piece of evidence was e-mailed across on Wednesday 4 May.

We made the deadline.

A GUINNESS WORLD
RECORDS RECORD
IS SET

Our Guinness World Records claims advisor called Ray on the Wednesday for verification of the figures quoted and for explanation of some of the terminology used and appeared satisfied by all she heard. Ray immediately called Ruth to tell her that she may be getting a good news telephone call soon!

On Thursday morning 5 May, Guinness World Record's press officer rang Ruth and me to tell us the good news: we had been awarded the title of 'World's loudest domestic purring cat'. It was official.

They just needed one more piece of information: would Ruth give them a quote for their famous book about how she felt about her experiences of achieving a Guinness World Records record for me?

'Shattered' sprang to mind, but Ruth said she would think about it and send them a quote in a few minutes. This is what she said via e-mail.

'Smokey and I are very excited at being awarded the Guinness World Records record for the Loudest Purring Domestic cat.

'We originally started a purring competition in our home town of Northampton in order to promote the cats' charity, Cats Protection, and we are totally overwhelmed with the news that she has been declared the World's loudest cat.

'We wish to thank all those whom have supported Smokey with her record attempt and especially wish to thank Northampton College for organising the trials and supplying the expertise I needed to comply with the technical aspects of a Guinness World Records record claim. We are very happy and purring loudly with pleasure at the announcement that we hold a World Record. Ruth Adams, owner of Smokey the Cat.

'At last! Ruth and Smokey'.

I was now officially famous. The story spread around the world again very quickly, and I performed further purr interviews for radio stations. I even did a Skype interview with New Zealand, but that did not go so well as I fell off my cushion halfway through my interview. Do I need all this stress?

A week later the Guinness World Records certificate arrived and I felt very proud. I sent Ruth out to find a suitable frame for it. A reunion of all my support crew was organised to meet at Northampton College so that they could all see and hold the certificate. I thought as this was the location where my world record attempt started it would be nice to have the finishing picture taken there. We were also very interested to see how the college's new buildings were shaping up.

Ruth contacted all those who had helped with our bid to find out who would be available at short notice to join us for a group picture. We all agreed to meet up at 12 noon on Friday 20 May at the college's reception area. The *Northampton Chronicle & Echo* newspaper had agreed to take the pictures and run a follow-on story.

Well, just like everything else in our story: expect the unexpected. Ruth and I set forth to the college heading up the farm's back drive towards the village, when we came across a loose brown pony grazing very hungrily at the lush grass at the edge of the drive. The pony belonged to a neighbour and so we immediately contacted the owner to let them know before continuing on our journey to the college. Predictably, as usual, we were late for the photo call.

We then parked in the totally wrong car park as the new building works had changed things temporarily. Aware that everyone would be waiting Ruth ran with me swinging alongside – I was not enjoying the bumpy ride. I arrived at the photograph session shaken but not stirred. Ruth, on the other hand, was breathing very heavily and her face was glowing bright red. So much for all the time spent trying to groom her hair to look nice, the time was wasted. Still smiling but not immaculate we joined the group pictures.

Following the picture session we were very honoured to be asked to become a mascot for the college. I accepted immediately. I wonder if I get an honorary diploma in animal management or something similar? I could even become a doctor. Even cats have dreams, usually about mice and encounters with fellow cats but then I am no ordinary cat: I am a Guinness World Records record-breaking Cat.

CAT FACT
When a cat swishes its tail back and forth, they are concentrating on something: if their tail starts moving faster, they have become annoyed.

CAT FACT
The life span of a well treated healthy cat could be up to 20 years or more.

My first 'meet the public' session was organised at a local veterinary centre in Market Harborough which was around 12 miles away. The Town and Country Veterinary Centre were having an open day to demonstrate their new animal hospital which they had recently opened. It all looked clean, clinical and very scary. As all animal owners know, the visit to the vets can be an alarming occasion for the animal patient, lots of strange smells and different animals, especially dogs. I felt reassured when we were greeted with the happy faces of the people who worked at the new centre; they were definitely all kind animal lovers. Being an important celebrity cat I was shown to my own private consulting/changing room to greet the visiting public. It was a very tiring afternoon making so many new friends but I enjoyed myself. I was concentrating so hard on my introductions that my purr facility did not work very well but I do not think my guests were disappointed. It is not every day you get to rub and stroke an international celebrity.

Midway through the afternoon we decided to venture out of our room and carry out a hospital inspection. The centre looked very new and impressive but I really do not want to visit as a patient as I simply do not have time to get old or be ill, but it is reassuring to know that the facility is there if I need to in the future.

I also noticed that they had a lot of posters warning about the dangers of over-feeding your cat. They had a small sample bowl showing your cat's daily allowance of dried biscuits. I was hoping that Ruth did not see this as it is half my normal ration. I DEFINATLEY DO NOT CONSIDER DIETS. I can't purr if I am starving. I needed to keep Ruth away from these 'health warnings' I wriggled in her arms as she walked past the bowl so that she would keep moving. I think I got away with it.

The next room was the dentistry room and operating theatre. This was equally scary. I have seen too many horror films on the television. I think I need a good dose of sedative or cat-nip to feel relaxed in here. I could not believe the array of equipment that they proudly had on display. I think, as a cat, that the place would look a lot better with a few brightly coloured scatter cushions around for us to snooze on. Inspection over we headed back to my consulting room and I finished the afternoon advising visitors how to make their cats happy.

CAT FACTS

Cats with white fur and skin on their noses and ears are very prone to sunburn which increases their risk of skin cancer. To help protect your white cat apply sunblock to their ears and nose or keep them inside on sunny days.

CAT FACT

Neutering a cat usually extends a male cat's life span by two or three years as they are less prone to straying and fighting.

CAT FACT

A large majority of white cats with blue eyes are deaf. White cats with only one blue eye are deaf only in the ear closest to the blue eye. White cats with orange eyes are usually not deaf.

Life now is getting back to normal and its usual routine. To meet me you would not know I had a secret, that is until I start purring. I am a little rehomed rescue cat with big dreams and loud voice. If I can have my five minutes of fame any one can. Go chase your dreams and be happy. I hope you enjoyed reading my story.

Keep Happy and Purring,
Love Smokey xxxx
The World's Loudest Purring Domestic Cat

Smokey

PS. Please remember to spay or neuter your cat if not used for breeding purposes.

Cat secures place in record books

Dedication pays off for our Smokey

SMOKEY looks like the cat that got the cream after being officially recognised for being the loudest on record.

By Daniel Owens
News Editor

daniel.owens@northantsnews.co.uk

Guinness World Records announced today that the 12-year-old female British short-hair cat achieved the loudest purr by a domestic cat, peaking at 67.7 dB.

Smokey's owner Ruth Adams, from Pitsford, near Northampton, said: "Smokey and I are very excited at being awarded the Guinness World Records title for the loudest purring domestic cat.

"We originally started a purring competition in Northampton to promote the cats charity Cats Protection.

"We wish to thank all those who have supported Smokey with her record attempt and especially wish to thank Northampton College for organising the trials and supplying the expertise I needed to comply with the technical aspects of a Guinness World Records claim.

"We are very happy and purring loudly at the announcement that we hold a Guinness World Records title."

Craig Glenday, editor-in-chief of Guinness World Records, said: "The book is a veritable cat-alogue of fantastic felines, and Smokey is a welcome addition to the family. It's incredible to think that a cat's purr can be as loud as a vacuum clean-er." Smokey, *pictured below*, still has a way to go to compete with the noisiest beasts in the animal kingdom.

The loudest animal sound is the low-frequency pulses made by blue whales and fin whales when communicating with each other.

These whales reach 188 dB on the decibel scale, creating the loudest sounds emitted by any living source.

Total silence is 0 dB, a lawnmower 90 dB, a car horn 110 dB and a rock concert 120 dB.

Northamptonshire Chronicle and Echo newspaper, Friday 6 May, 2011.

WHAT IS SOUND AND HOW IS SOUND MEASURED?

The scientific bit – What is sound?

'**Sound is a type of energy made by invisible vibrations.**'
The origin of the sound may be a telephone, car horn, or loud purring cat but, whatever it is, some part of it must be vibrating to produce a sound wave. When the source of the sound vibrates, it bumps into the tiny particles called molecules in the air next to it, which then bump into other molecules. These movements are called **sound waves** and they will keep going until they run out of energy.

Sound waves need to travel through **a medium** like air, water or solid material to reach the ear. If your ear is within range of the **vibrations**, you hear the sound. Our ears pick up these sound waves and send messages to the brain to convert them into sound. The smallest bone in the human body is found in the ear. It is called the Stapes. It is only 0.25cm to 0.33cm long.

Why do we need to measure sound?

People can never agree on how loud any noise is and so to compare noise levels an accurate measure has to be taken of the strength of the sound waves. The strength of a sound wave is measured using a decibel meter.

The decibel (dB for short) is the unit used to measure the intensity of sound. The decibel scale is a little odd because an ear is incredibly sensitive. You can hear anything from a rustling leaf to a jet engine.

All decibel readings are taken usually at a standard distance of **1 metre away from the sound source,** as the closer you are to the source the louder it will appear to be.

Here are some examples of decibel readings

A whisper 15dB

A ticking watch 20dB

Normal Purring Cat 25dB*

Normal conversation 50-60dB

Smokey Purring Cat 67.7dB

Car Traffic 70dB

Alarm Clock 80dB

Lawn Mower 90dB

Pain for human ear 120-130dB

Jet engine 140dB

*figure supplied by Bav media and associated content from Yahoo Oct 2008.

Decibels are logarithmic, so for every 3dB increase in sound measured the intensity of the sound increases by a further multiple. This is done because the ranges of numbers a human ear can detect are so vast. If a normal cat purred at 25dB and then increased her purring to 40dB this would mean that she was purring at a level five times louder than before. If the same cat then notched her purring up to 55dB she would then be 10 times louder than her starting purr. If she really felt like an operatic diva and registered a purr at 70dB she would be purring at a rate 15 times louder than she normally sang.

Hence when Smokey purred at 67.7dB she is purring at a level which is 14 times louder than the 'average' cat's reading.

Do humans and animals hear different things?

Animals and humans can hear different ranges of sound.

A cat can hear a far greater range of sounds, which our ears find it impossible to hear. They can detect the precise direction of a sound and can distinguish between two sounds that are only 18in apart at a distance of 60ft. Cats hear sounds at great distances – four or five times further away than humans. A cat up to 3ft away from the origin of a sound can pinpoint its location to within a few centimetres in a mere six one-hundredths of a second. So when you are calling your pussy cat in the garden, she probably can hear you but is choosing to pretend she can't. Cats use their whiskers to sense and feel vibrations, and they have excellent eyesight especially at night. Cats have better hearing than dogs.

The best hearing award from my small survey I award to Mr Bat. As bats are virtually blind they navigate at night by sound. They find tasty moths to eat by emitting high pitch noises which then bounce back to them when they hit something. This is called echo location.

The world's noisiest animal on land is the Howler Monkey of South America. Their calls can be heard five kilometres away.

Another very noisy animal is the Blue Whale and is the largest mammal alive today. Blue Whales sing by emitting a very loud repetitive low-frequency rumbling song that can travel for many hundreds of kilometres under water. These songs are used to talk to their friends and find a partner. At least this saves on expensive mobile telephone or text bills!

The prize for the loudest animal is awarded to the very small Pistol Shrimp. This emits a sound of 218dB in the water to stun its dinner. This is similar to the noise level of a Concorde.

How fast can sound waves travel? and other facts
At a temperature of 68F (20C) sound travels through air at 1,125ft (343 metres) per second. This is the same as travelling at 756mph (1,217 kph).

Objects moving faster than this are said to be supersonic. A fast aeroplane can go faster than the speed of sound. When this happens a loud boom is heard called a sonic boom.

As the temperature rises, the speed of sound gets faster.

Light, however, travels far quicker through air or water than sound. **Light can travel at 671 million mph (or 1,080 million kph).** This means you may see things before you hear them, for example it may take a few seconds after seeing a flash of lightening until you hear the thunder.

Sound measurements can be used for other things other than to do with hearing. These include: helping to detect oil, gas and mineral reserves, providing information to boats about the sea bed and even providing expectant mothers with a picture of their unborn child.

Why and how do cats purr?

It is usually thought that a cat will purr when it is happy or contented; however, this is not always true. Sometimes a cat will use purring as a way to release tension or stress it is feeling. A cat in pain visiting the vet may well be purring, not from pleasure, but as a way of trying to relax and ask for help.

It has been found that cats can have different types of purring. When a cat is hungry or first thing in the morning the cat may greet its owner with a more shrill demanding 'feed me right now' type of purr, while in an evening, when say on your lap the purring is far more relaxed. Smokey has developed the art of the loud demanding purr to the extreme.

A purr is a two-way sound as the cat breathes in and out. Large cats like lions and tigers cannot purr. However, they can roar, which is perhaps not as relaxing as a purr if one was to sit on your knee!

There are two theories as to how a cat can purr and scientists cannot actually agree. The first explanation is that the cat has an extra 'false' set of vocal cords within its voice box and this creates the purr sound through vibrations. The other suggestion is that the purring is a result of turbulence in the blood pressure as it is pushed through the cat's chest. For this theory to be true a cat's blood pressure would increase when it purred and not reduce. Whichever description of these is the correct one the cat population are keeping it a secret and not letting the 'men in white coats' know.

The end,
Good bye
Ruth Adams
and ✗ Smokey